HOME MADE

Cooking at home with Melbourne's
best cooks, chefs and restaurants

A BOOK BY

◉ BROADSHEET

Photography by Mark Roper
Art Direction and Design by The Company You Keep

HOME MADE

Featuring:

Abla Amad, Abla's

Adam D'Sylva, Coda and Tonka

Alejandro Saravia, Pastuso

Almay Jordaan, Old Palm Liquor

Andreas Papadakis, Osteria Ilaria

Andrew McConnell, Trader House Restaurants

Angie Giannakodakis, Epocha

Ash Smith, Stokehouse

Benjamin Cooper, Chin Chin

Brigitte Hafner, Tedesca Osteria

Caelan O'Rourke, Raphael Hyams and Geoff Marett, Nama

Chavalit Piyaphanee, Soi 38

Colin Mainds, Cutler & Co.

Dan Hunter, Brae

Dani Valent

Dani Zeini, Royal Stacks

Dave Verheul, Embla

David Zhou, Oriental Teahouse and David's

Dawit Kebede, Mesob

Dougal Colam, Bhang

Eileen Horsnell, Napier Quarter

Ernest Tovar, Nómada

Frank Camorra, Movida

Gareth Whitton, Tarts Anon

Geraud Fabre, France-Soir

Guy Grossi, Grossi Florentino

Hana Assafiri, Moroccan Soup Bar

Hugh Allen, Vue de Monde

Jamie Valmorbida and Luca Sbardella, King & Godfree

Jarrod Di Blasi, Izakaya Den 2029

Jesse Gerner, Bomba

Jessi Singh, Daughter in Law

Joey Kellock, 1800 Lasagne

Joseph Abboud, Rumi

Julia Busuttil Nishimura

Julian Hills, Navi

Karina Serex, Tuck Shop Take Away

Kay-Lene Tan, Coda and Tonka

Khanh Nguyen, Sunda

Koichi Minamishima and Yoshiki Tano, Minamishima

Konstandakopoulos family, Stalactites

Lisa Valmorbida, Pidapipó

Marco Finanzio, Umberto Espresso Bar

Matt Lane, Mamasita

Matt McConnell, Bar Lourinhā

Michael Bacash, Bacash

Michael Li, Super Ling

Michael Madrusan, The Everleigh

Mike Russell and John Paul Twomey, Baker Bleu

Nam Nguyen, Good Days

Nick Deligiannis, Frédéric

Philip and Shirley Leong, Gai Wong

Philippe Mouchel, Philippe

Tanpapat family, Jinda Thai

Raph Rashid, Beatbox Kitchen

Rita Macali, Supermaxi

Rosheen Kaul, Etta

Roy Sassonkin, Tahina

Roystan Leow, Mr Ramen San

Scott Pickett, Estelle

Shane Delia, Maha

Shannon Martinez, Smith & Daughters

Shiyamalee Somaweera, Citrus

Thi Le, Anchovy

Tom Sarafian, Bar Saracen

Tony Tan, Tony Tan Cooking School

Victor Liong, Lee Ho Fook

Ying Hou and Meiyan Wang, Shandong Mama

Casa Iberica, Fitzroy

CONTENTS

INTRODUCTION

It might be an obvious thing to say that professional chefs don't really cook like the rest of us. On top of being formally trained, they have a whole layer of tips, tricks and instincts built up over years and years of cooking meal after meal for thousands of people.

I'd always understood this in a vague, abstract kind of way. But in 2020 we got to see that firsthand and up close. While we were all stuck inside, chefs began inviting us into their homes through YouTube and Instagram. We got an unfiltered look at how they cook for themselves and their families – something scripted cooking shows have never really managed to capture properly.

It was a moment of clarity for me. I began to appreciate, on a practical level, just how differently chefs do things.

Most of us never really learn how to cook. Not properly. Not having someone who really knows what they're talking about stand next to us and teach us. Spending weeks and weeks making the same dish again and again in a high-pressure restaurant kitchen. Perfecting our knife skills through hundreds of hours of prep, chopping thousands of onions. Then moving to the larder section for hundreds more hours, then maybe the grill from there. It takes years of practice, repetition and mentoring for the chefs we admire to master their craft. Along the way, they get caught out mid-service and they graft their way out. Now that's a way to learn a few tricks.

The rest of us make do with learning what we can from parents, grandparents, housemates, boyfriends or girlfriends, who don't always know what they're talking about in the first place. Then of course, we read cookbooks and watch clips on online. That, together with a bit of interest, a touch of passion and enough hours over a stove, is the osmosis we need to start becoming pretty good home cooks. Maybe.

So after a year of watching these chefs cook for their families and their followers, we thought: let's create a book in that spirit. A book of the essential home recipes everyone should have in their repertoire. A book full of tips, tricks and advice that come from a place of real knowledge and experience.

→

And who better to share all this than 70 of Melbourne's best chefs?

Because there's baked flounder, and then there's Michael Bacash's baked flounder (page 115). There's weeknight pasta, and then there's Andrew McConnell's weeknight pasta (page 138).

And yes, there's roast chicken here, too. Now, you probably already know how to roast a chicken. But perhaps not like Philippe Mouchel (page 221).

For the most part, the recipes in *Home Made* are essential to their respective cuisines. As much as possible, we opted for classic, iconic dishes. But not just any version of these dishes, the *ultimate* versions, according to the chefs who've spent years – decades, even – thinking about and refining them. Some are quick, such as Joseph Abboud's smoky baba ganoush (page 43). Others are more complicated, such as Hugh Allen's decadent lamington (page 280), which will take all day but floor anyone who tastes it.

Though some of these dishes can be found at restaurants around town, this book is not about replicating restaurant food at home. These are dishes specifically for home.

We started by asking chefs two questions: "What do you cook when you're cooking for the people you love?" and "When you cook lasagne (or pho, or yellow curry, or another staple dish) at home, what do you bring to it that the average home cook wouldn't?"

Those two questions are the premise at the heart of this book, which is about getting to know the principles of professional cooking, to help you make better, more delicious food for yourself and the people you love. We call it "cheffiness". It's the difference between the way chefs and non-chefs cook at home.

Throughout these pages you'll find numerous tips and pieces of advice scattered about. You'll learn, for example, which kitchen utensils are worth spending serious money on, and which you can pick up at little cost (page 95). Or the genius secrets to organising your pantry (page 130). Even which spirits and equipment you need to start a home bar (page 251).

Home Made epitomises the spirit of Melbourne now. It's a cross-section of the culinary diversity and creativity that makes this such an inspiring city to live and eat in. It captures the warmth, optimism and community that's palpable in the streets. But more than anything, it celebrates a renewed appreciation for sharing a meal and a drink with the people we love.

Nick Shelton, *Broadsheet* founder and publisher

MENU

At heart, this is a book about cooking for, and eating with, the people you love. Whether it's a quick weeknight dinner for two or a Saturday-night dinner party for eight, these menus are designed to inspire and guide you. Use them as a starting point, but we encourage you to riff and improvise. The key to a good menu is that the dishes both complement and play off each other. A good meal tells a story.

Left: Pork and prawn siu mai, page 77; Middle: Drunken pipis with rolled rice
noodles and ginger chicken fat, page 64; Right: Zucchini dumplings, page 45

CHINESE, PLEASE

Fried rice, dim sum and other Cantonese specialities have been eaten in Australia since the 1800s. More recently, we've become acquainted with the spicy, numbing dishes of Sichuan, the seafood of Shandong, and the various flavours of other regions. What we once understood as "Chinese" is at least eight distinct cuisines, and as a trip to Box Hill, Glen Waverley or Chinatown will reveal, they showcase enormous diversity in technique and ingredients. Here's a small yet delicious sample, from Shanghai-style dumplings to addictive Chongqing noodles.

ZUCCHINI DUMPLINGS P.45

Ying Hou and Meiyan Wang, Shandong Mama

– AND –

PORK AND PRAWN SIU MAI P.77

David Zhou, David's and Oriental Teahouse

Make these delicious parcels in advance and pop them in the steamer once your guests arrive. Or make an afternoon of it and get your friends to join in making them.

DRUNKEN PIPIS WITH ROLLED RICE NOODLES AND GINGER CHICKEN FAT P.64

Victor Liong, Lee Ho Fook

– AND –

CHONGQING NOODLES P.93

Shannon Martinez, Smith & Daughters

Make these two very different noodle dishes (one vegan) for mains and you'll keep everyone happy. Just play it safe with the chilli and Sichuan pepper in the Chongqing noodles You can always add more spice, but you can't take it away.

MANGIAMO!

With its emphasis on fresh seasonal produce treated simply, Italian cuisine is a strong foundation for any home cook, regardless of how you like to eat. Whether you're shopping for Parmigiano Reggiano, broccoli or canned tomatoes, search out the highest-quality ingredients. Being so integral to Melbourne's culinary identity, Italian is also a safe bet when you're having a few people round. Mangiamo!

STRACCIATELLA, WALNUT AND CIME DI RAPA P.49

Dave Verheul, Embla

Start with "a little savoury Neapolitan", consisting of silky cheese, earthy walnut pesto and bitter greens melted in olive oil. Pair with a vermouth on ice, with a slice of your favourite citrus. Dave has his own seasonal vermouth brand, Saison, available at good independent bottle shops.

LINGUINE WITH FROMAGE FRAIS P.90

Eileen Horsnell, Napier Quarter

This light goat's cheese pasta makes a beautiful vegetarian mid-course, and you can add anchovies for a pungent, umami kick. Do as Eileen suggests and get your guests to help you roll out fresh pasta.

BISTECCA ALLA FIORENTINA P.245

Andreas Papadakis, Osteria Ilaria

A giant steak is always a show stopper. Pair with Andreas's charred broccolini, macadamia and capers (page 271).

BREAD AND BUTTER PUDDING WITH FIOR DI LATTE GELATO P.279

Lisa Valmorbida, Pidapipó

Finish with this simple crowd-pleasing dessert, and a bitter digestivo such as amaro. There are several excellent Australian amari now: Økar, Autonomy and Poor Tom's, to name a few.

THE LEVANT

The Levant encompasses Syria, Lebanon, Palestine, Israel, Jordan and Cyprus. All of these nations' colourful, contrast-rich cuisines are represented in Melbourne, but none is more abundant than Lebanese. Without it we wouldn't be nearly as familiar with ingredients such as tahini and sumac. And hummus probably wouldn't be available in supermarkets.

BABA GANOUSH P.43

Joseph Abboud, Rumi

– AND –

BARBEQUED CHICKEN WINGS WITH TOUM P.41

Joseph Abboud, Rumi

Warm up your barbeque and make some smoky dip and charry, garlicky chicken wings. Pass both around, or leave on a side table for people to serve themselves.

BAKED SALMON WITH TARATOR AND BURNT BUTTER P.132

Shane Delia, Maha

When it's time to sit down, this whole fish will make an outsized splash, courtesy of clever little tricks such as burnt butter infused with coffee grounds. Not to mention the colourful tabouli (page 268) it's covered with.

GOAT'S CHEESE MAMOOLS P.305

Tom Sarafian, Bar Saracen

These goat's cheese-filled biscuits, served with fig jam, are the perfect midway point between a cheese board and a dessert. Prep them ahead of time and bake fresh.

DIY WINE BAR

A little bit snacky, a little bit fancy, a little bit European. Melbourne's wine bars have developed a style that stretches well beyond a few salty snacks. Nowadays they're just as likely to serve dinner as they are olives and charcuterie. Bring the experience home with this menu.

SNAPPER CEVICHE P.39

Alejandro Saravia, Pastuso

– AND –

STRACCIATELLA, WALNUT AND CIME DI RAPA P.49

Dave Verheul, Embla

– AND –

JAMON AND LEEK CROQUETAS P.71

Ernest Tovar, Nómada

Pass these small plates around while you pour everyone an apéritif. Take your time: in this world, a meal can be nothing but snacks and pre-drinks.

CIDER-BRINED PORK CHOPS P.233

Almay Jordaan, Old Palm Liquor

– AND –

PEA SALAD WITH PICKLED SHALLOTS P.268

Almay Jordaan, Old Palm Liquor

– AND –

CHARRED BROCCOLINI, MACADAMIA AND CAPERS P.271

Andreas Papadakis, Osteria Ilaria

A simple, delicious main is what we're going for here. Allow one or two pork chops per person and serve the sides on a platter.

CHOCOLATE AND CARAMEL TART P.296

Gareth Whitton, Tarts Anon

Make it an elegant finish with this tart, paired with a good dessert wine, or a cheeky champagne.

★ BON APPÉTIT ★

Confit. Sous vide. Mise en place. Where would the world be without the French and their carefully refined techniques? Not to mention their structured, hierarchical kitchens, a system which underpins every Western restaurant. Bring a bit of this order, care and sheer reverence for food into your house and see how quickly you reap the benefits. A simple steak with butter becomes heavenly.

SWEETCORN AND ESPELETTE MADELEINES P.68

Nick Deligiannis, Frédéric

This savoury take on the classic shell-shaped cake is a moreish entry to any meal. Allow two or three per person, plus a glass or two of champagne.

WHOLE ROAST DUCK WITH ORANGE P.230

Brigitte Hafner, Tedesca Osteria

Served fresh from the oven, roast duck is a proper show stopper. If you're thinking summer lunch, Philippe Mouchel's roast chicken (page 221) can't be beaten.

– OR –

BOEUF BOURGUIGNON P.241

Geraud Fabre, France-Soir

If it's the dead of winter, go for this classic beef stew. Get it bubbling away several hours before you're due to eat. It can sit on the stove, keeping warm, while everyone enjoys the entrees.

PEAR TARTE TATIN P.285

Dan Hunter, Brae

Classics don't get much better than this, which emerges from under the pan in a cloud of theatrical – and deliciously scented – steam. The pastry must be prepared the day before, but the final step is just an hour in the oven.

Left: Adjard pickles, page 258; Bottom right: Yellow Curry, page 150; Top right: Som tum, page 258

FOLLOW THE MEKONG

Pungent fish sauce. Fiery chilli. Zingy lime. Contrast and vibrancy are prized on both sides of the immense Mekong River, which runs through Thailand and Vietnam as well as China, Laos, Myanmar and Cambodia. This maximalist approach works because the local chefs have such a fine understanding of balance. They know how to play salty, spicy, sour and sweet against one another. Taste frequently, adjust frequently, and you'll get there too.

BANH MI P.61

Thi Le, Anchovy

Banh mi is not just for lunch. Make pork meatballs ahead of time, then put them on a buffet-style table with halved or quartered baguettes, mayo, pickled veggies and cucumber. Your friends can help themselves.

YELLOW CURRY P.150

Benjamin Cooper, Chin Chin

This versatile curry works well with any type of seafood, meat or veggies. Put a range of pre-cooked options on the table – everyone can spoon the curry sauce over to make their own plate.

ADJARD PICKLES P.258

Benjamin Cooper, Chin Chin

– AND –

SOM TUM P.258

Tanpapat family, Jinda Thai

Round out the meal with these refreshing sides that still pack a full-flavoured punch.

Karaage chicken ribs, page 52

ITADAKIMASU

From the CBD's boisterous izakayas to the droves of suburban sushi trains and ramen shops, Melbourne is flush when it comes to Japanese food. Eat at any of these restaurants and you'll notice an enthusiasm for umami, or savouriness – the fifth basic taste after sweet, salty, sour and bitter. Learn to harness it and you'll be on your way to mastering Japanese food.

KARAAGE CHICKEN RIBS P.52

Jarrod Di Blasi, Izakaya Den 2029

– AND –

EBI TOAST P.53

Caelan O'Rourke, Raphael Hyams
and Geoff Marett, Nama

Kick off your night with these moreish, izakaya-style snacks and a few bottles of crisp Japanese beer. Prep both dishes ahead of time.

FISH COLLAR NABE P.144

Koichi Minamishima and Yoshiki Tano, Minamishima

Move onto a bottle of your favourite sake and a big, hearty pot of fish stew, courtesy of the city's best sushi chef and his right-hand man.

FRUIT COBBLER P.288

Kay-Lene Tan, Coda and Tonka

This generous, highly shareable fruit pie can be made with whatever fruit you have on hand. But for this menu, opt for Fuji apples, nashi pears or another Japanese variety.

REAL ESPAÑA

Sitting outdoors, eating something delicious with people you love – this is the essence of Spanish food. We're well set up to take advantage of it in Melbourne, in backyards and on balconies if nothing else. If you're drinking, make up a big sloshing jug of sangria, or push the boat out with a sherry or an interesting wine variety such as sparkling cava, peach-y white albariño or ruby red tempranillo. Whatever quenches your thirst.

PIQUILLO PEPPERS ON TOAST P.70

John Paul Twomey, Baker Bleu

– AND –

JAMON AND LEEK CROQUETAS P.71

Ernest Tovar, Nómada

Go heavy on these drinking-friendly snacks and leave several hours before mains, for everyone to really work up an appetite – it's what the Spanish would do.

SPANISH MACKEREL MARINATED IN ANDALUSIAN SPICES P.119

Frank Camorra, Movida

– AND –

CHICKEN PAELLA WITH PIPIS P.189

Jesse Gerner, Bomba

It might be 10 or even 11pm by the time you serve these two shareable mains, and that's fine. You're on Spanish time now. The mackerel needs to be prepared the day before and fried fresh – a job you can entrust to one guest while you handle the paella on the stove, right next to them.

Left: Kashmiri paneer, page 106; Middle: Tadka,
page 209; Right: Tamarind eggplant, page 257

FROM

THE

SUBCONTINENT

It shouldn't surprise anyone to learn that India grows three-quarters of the world's spices. From masala chai to samosas, panipuri to korma, the cuisine (and that of neighbouring Sri Lanka) is defined by a heady, complex use of spices. Buying fresh from a specialty grocer with regular turnover is a must if you want to make high-definition curries and other dishes.

KASHMIRI PANEER P.106

Dougal Colam, Bhang

– AND –

RED LENTIL CURRY P.89

Shiyamalee Somaweera, Citrus

Don't worry about separate courses here. Just prepare everything in advance, then heat and put on the table with steamed basmati rice, naan, roti or another bread, and your favourite condiments.

TADKA P.209

Jessi Singh, Daughter in Law

– AND –

TAMARIND EGGPLANT P.257

Rosheen Kaul, Etta

Tadka is the base for countless Indian-style curries that you can jazz up with fish, prawns, goat, beef or any other protein or vegetables you like.

WEEKNIGHT WINNERS

Everyone needs a back catalogue of quick, easy recipes to call on
at the end of a tough day. Try one of these – all use widely available
ingredients and come together with minimal time and effort.

RED LENTIL CURRY P.89

Shiyamalee Somaweera, Citrus

A big pot of this takes 30 minutes to make and
feeds a household of any size, with plenty left
over for lunches the next day. Plus, it uses almost
nothing but affordable, non-perishable ingredients.

LINGUINE WITH FROMAGE FRAIS AND FENNEL P.90

Eileen Horsnell, Napier Quarter

This spring goat's cheese number works
all year round. If you're craving extra
savouriness, swap the olives for anchovies.

CHONGQING NOODLES P.93

Shannon Martinez, Smith & Daughters

You'll need to shop ahead for specialty
ingredients such as tian mian jiang (sweet bean
paste) and doubanjiang (fermented chilli bean
paste), but once you have everything, these
numbing noodles are on the table in 30 minutes.

MINESTRONE P.99

Rita Macali, Supermaxi

This minestrone needs an hour to
simmer, but you can be on the couch
most of the time. And at the end, you
get a hearty, veggie-packed bowl of
comfort. Win-win.

CHICKPEA BAKE P.100

Hana Assafiri, Moroccan Soup Bar

Got yoghurt, canned chickpeas
and some spare flatbread?
You've got a quick and
filling dinner.

TROTTOLE PASTA, PRAWNS, TOMATO AND TARRAGON P.138

Andrew McConnell, Trader House Restaurants

In the mood for pasta? Andrew McConnell's,
featuring a quick prawn stock and refined
herby finish, packs maximum flavour.

NASI GORENG P.156

Raph Rashid, Beatbox Kitchen

Clear out your fridge or pantry with
this adaptable fried rice, which can be
tricked out with hot sauce, fried eggs,
pickled ginger and/or whatever's left
in your veggie crisper.

TADKA P.209

Jessi Singh, Daughter in Law

Keep a big batch of this wonderfully
versatile curry base in the freezer, and you
can whip it out next time you're stuck for
ideas. It can be bulked up with pretty much
any meat or vegetables you like.

WEEKEND PROJECTS

Often, cooking is as much about the journey as it is the destination. Sometimes you want to spend a whole day shopping, prepping and cooking. In those times, you need recipes like these.

CIOPPINO WITH MUSSELS AND ROCK FLATHEAD P.141

Colin Mainds, Cutler & Co.

Packed with mussels, pipis, calamari and fish, this fragrant tomato-based stew is the Italian–American answer to bouillabaisse. Put aside three hours to make it happen.

KYUSHU-STYLE CHASHU TONKOTSU RAMEN P.161

Roystan Leow, Mr Ramen San

Tonkotsu ramen can take two or even three full days to make. If you have a pressure cooker, this abridged (yet totally legit) version is ready in a mere six hours, which you can spread out over multiple days.

BEEF PHO P.167

Nam Nguyen, Good Days

This complex, aromatic pho is inspired by ramen and employs similar techniques. The difference is in the flavours: ginger, coriander, cloves, star anise and cassia are the stars of this soup.

BOAT NOODLES P.170

Chavalit Piyaphanee, Soi 38

Thai boat noodles may be less famous than Vietnamese pho, but the dish offers similar thrills: a heady, comforting broth packed with noodles and tender slices of meat. Allow six hours to bring it to fruition.

LASAGNE P.185

Joey Kellock, 1800 Lasagne

Clocking in at nearly seven hours, this is definitely the most painstaking lasagne you'll ever make. But we're fairly confident it will also be the best. The ragu alone is worth the time.

DORO WAT P.200

Dawit Kebede, Mesob

You need patience to cook this chicken stew, the national dish of Ethiopia, which involves sauteeing onions for more than two hours. But when all's said and done, this buttery, lemon-y delight will feel more than worth it.

HAINANESE CHICKEN RICE P.212

Philip and Shirley Leong, Gai Wong

HCR looks simple, but the delicate poached bird is a real labour of love, taking at least three hours to prepare. Make sure to use a good-quality chicken.

LAMINGTONS P.280

Hugh Allen, Vue de Monde

Give this Aussie classic the respect and meticulous attention it's so long been denied, while sitting in plastic packets on supermarket shelves. You'll never see it the same way again.

Mapo tofu jaffle, page 33

SUPPER TIME

Heading out? Know you'll be home late, hungry and possibly with company? Plan ahead to make one of these salty, carb-y, hangover-averting numbers.

MAPO TOFU JAFFLE P.33

Michael Li, Super Ling

Prepare the pork and tofu filling ahead of time – when you get home, just whack it in the jaffle-maker between two slices of buttered bread and you're set.

EBI TOAST P.53

Caelan O'Rourke, Raphael Hyams and Geoff Marett, Nama

If you're feeling fit for deep-frying, try this umami-packed, golden fried toast, originally conceived during a drunken 2am conversation.

PIQUILLO PEPPERS ON TOAST P.70

John Paul Twomey, Baker Bleu

If you're still drinking good wine and still feeling on top of the world, this goat's cheese toast is the snack to beat.

NASI GORENG P.156

Raph Rashid, Beatbox Kitchen

Fried rice? You know you want it.

City of my Heart

By Dani Valent,
cook, author and food writer

The first avocado I ate was under a gum tree, in a park, near the Royal Botanic Gardens. It was transformative, like an initiation. I was maybe 11 and it was the early 1980s. I had finished my afternoon newspaper delivery round and coins jangled in my pocket. On my way to the milk bar for musk Lifesavers and an icy pole, I stopped at the fruit shop, drawn in by glossy avocados arranged in neat tissue-papered rows. It was the first time I'd seen them. We had apples, bananas and oranges in the fruit bowl at home, and grapes in the fridge. The closest I'd come to an avocado was the picture of a prawn cocktail in my mum's fancy dinner-party cookbook.

Possibly I was the weirdest grade sixer in Melbourne, but I bought a single avocado with my paper round money and took it to the park across the road. I had no idea how to eat it. Standing on the grass in the shade, I dug my newsprinted thumbnail into the avocado's skin and started peeling it. Avocados don't neatly reveal themselves but eventually I exposed enough two-tone green to put my teeth into it, taking my first soft, scraping bite. It was a revelation. I remember trying to describe it to myself. Tree butter. Green lard. Fruit cream. I kept going, lost in it, eating my way deeper into flavour and texture, getting messy because avocados don't crunch cleanly like apples. I found the stone, slipped my way around it. It was an awed, mashed, smashed entry into taste adventures.

I had an inkling then about food being a good way to tumble myself out of the everyday and into newness.

I felt it again when I ate my first pho at Thy Thy on Victoria Street, watching other diners to glean what to do with the plate of garnishes. Tentatively, I pulled basil and mint from the stalk, squeezed lime, added chilli, scattered bean shoots. And dove in. There was something so generous about being served a dish I had no idea about and being trusted to finish it to my own taste, as though I had any. I loved the feeling of falling into the broth and even now, face in pho, I am flooded with the privilege of connecting to people, place and culture through the artlessly human need to eat.

People eat everywhere and waves of migration wash over many cities, but there are elements to Melbourne that make it truly special. It's physical: fertile soil stretches back from a fine bay, there's plenty of fresh water and a moderate climate that might not always scream "picnic" but usually keeps plants pushing skyward. And this place feeds us. We're still connected to our food bowl in a way that many cities around the world aren't. Almost half the food eaten here is grown within a couple of hours' drive.

Mineral bounty spurred Melbourne too. The city grew big and proud on the riches of the mid-19th century Gold Rush and the easy grandeur of the city's commercial buildings and boulevards still hasn't rubbed away. You see it in the pubs too, with their big verandas and curlicues of wrought iron, built for everyone. My first job, post-paper round, was in a pub kitchen, opening tins of three-bean mix for the salad bar and burying myself to the armpit to wash dirty soup pots. After I clocked off, I'd hang around and revel in the camaraderie and cacophony: cheering another goal for Carlton, sticky carpet keeping my happy feet planted, kids playing chasey in the throng. It was in restaurants that I first pretended to be grown up, sitting in the back room at Pellegrini's with a tumbler of wine, shocked and proud to see my red lipstick imprint on the rim. A few years later, while not really studying law, I sat at the window bench at Marios Cafe on Brunswick Street, Fitzroy, eating spaghetti with salmon and vodka sauce, feeling philosophical and sophisticated, ready to take on the world.

So I did. I saved up, lugged a backpack from one continent to the next. Remember those easy passport-stamping days? Coming home was never boring, not least because new Melburnians also brought fresh flavours to my hometown: nixtamalised corn for tortillas, teff to make injera, gai lan for stir-fries, sweet and salty jamon. There's also been a stuttering reckoning with the food that was always here: saltbush, mussels, wattleseed, wallaby, a native pantry trampled and hampered by our city, calling to be honoured once more. Avocado, needless to say, has become ubiquitous.

Since I was about eight, I answered the nosy, boring, "What do you want to be?" question with "Writer." I loved stories. I liked reading everything from plumbing catalogues to Russian novels to the footy record. It was by chance that I started working at travel publisher Lonely Planet, in Hawthorn. They needed invoicing done, and a friend roped me in to help for a few days.

Soon, I'd elbowed my way across the corridor from bookshop liaison to travel authoring and was able to hoik backpack onto shoulder again: Bulgaria, India, New York, wherever, I never doubted that Melbourne was home. Coming back always feels like a puzzle piece slotting back in: it's the taste of the water, the sound of the trams, the xiao long bao queue shuffle, the MCG sirens, the pilgrimage for the next perfect coffee. When Lonely Planet started a series of restaurant guides, I found myself on the Japanese beat, eating my way around Melbourne for my first food-writing foray. Nasu dengaku – miso-glazed eggplant – became my control dish, something I ordered in each of 20 Japanese restaurants, ranking it for softness, sweetness and salty funkiness. I loved the opportunities: to explore neighbourhoods, uncover stories and – of course – eat.

That was 20 years and two million words ago. I'm more than ever enamoured of Melbourne, city of my heart. Even – and especially – through the pandemic, I kept unwrapping the gift of connecting: Gujarati breads at Helly Raichura's Enter Via Laundry, Jakarta-style beef from Mangan Yuk, babka from Babka Boi, cacio e pepe tortellini from Al Dente, guacamole – that other smashed avocado – from Radio Mexico: all portals to tradition and deep emotion.

I love writing about food because I love writing about people: I get to talk to them, ask them dumb questions, and weave the answers into stories where – hopefully – they see themselves. These are my little stitches on the quilt of connection that we create together. It covers Melbourne, keeps us cosy and makes this such a special place to eat our way to ourselves.

SNACK
& STAR

KS
TERS

GREEN FALAFEL
ROY SASSONKIN, TAHINA

Prep time 30 minutes, plus overnight soaking and 30 minutes resting

Cook time 20 minutes

Makes 24 falafels

Growing up in Tel Aviv, Israel, I was spoilt for choice when it came to quality falafel. I never thought about making my own until I moved to Melbourne in 2012 and experienced cravings for one of my favourite childhood foods. I tried many variations before I landed on this recipe, which makes a fresh and zesty falafel that is moist on the inside and crunchy on the outside. At Tahina, we serve these falafels on top of salads, stuffed into pita pockets or on their own.

250g dried chickpeas

1 tsp baking powder

½ large brown onion roughly chopped

9 cloves garlic finely chopped

½ bunch parsley leaves picked and finely chopped

½ bunch coriander leaves picked and finely chopped

½ bunch mint leaves picked and finely chopped

1 tbsp sea salt

½ tsp freshly ground black pepper

1 tsp ground cumin

1 tsp ground coriander

½ tsp chilli flakes

Vegetable oil for shallow-frying

CHOPPED SALAD

4 ripe tomatoes deseeded and diced

4 Lebanese cucumbers diced

1 red onion diced

½ bunch parsley leaves picked and finely chopped

½ bunch coriander leaves picked and finely chopped

½ bunch mint leaves picked and finely chopped

1 clove garlic finely chopped

2 tbsp lemon juice

3 tbsp extra-virgin olive oil

Salt flakes and freshly ground black pepper to taste

Place the chickpeas in a large bowl and cover with cold water. Stir through the baking powder, then set aside in the fridge to soak overnight. The baking powder allows the chickpeas to soften, resulting in smoother, creamier falafels.

The next day, drain and rinse the chickpeas, then place in a food processor and pulse for 15 seconds. Scrape down the side of the bowl, then pulse for another 15 seconds. Repeat this method until the chickpeas are finely chopped but not mushy.

Add the onion, garlic, herbs, salt and spices to the food processor and pulse the mixture until it is coarsely chopped, but not pureed (the texture should look like cooked couscous and will hold its shape if rolled into a ball).

Place the falafel mixture in a bowl, then cover and set aside in the fridge for at least 1.5 hours to firm up.

To shape the falafels, use a falafel scoop or a tablespoon to divide the mixture into 30g balls. Gently use the palms of your hands to roll each ball and perfect its shape. Continue with the remaining mixture to make 24 falafels.

Pour vegetable oil into a large frying pan to a depth of 2.5cm, then heat over medium–high heat to 190°C on a kitchen thermometer. Working in batches, gently place the falafels in the pan using a slotted spoon and cook for about 2 minutes each side, until brown and crisp on the outside.

Drain the falafels on paper towel to remove excess oil.

To make the salad, add all the ingredients to a large bowl, mix together and add salt and pepper to taste. Serve the falafels on top.

Snacks & Starters

MAPO TOFU JAFFLE
MICHAEL LI, SUPER LING

Prep time 10 minutes

Cook time 20–25 minutes

Serves 6

I borrowed from a few people for this recipe. James Viles from Biota Dining in Bowral, NSW, did a pop-up in Melbourne and served a jaffle with bolognese sauce and cheese. It kind of opened up to me what you can do with food. And I like having jaffles at home, so I got excited about the idea of changing that into an Asian dish. The tofu was something I learned from Lee Ho Fook and the mapo came from researching recipes on the internet and mixing and matching everything I found. I never expected it to become Super Ling's bestselling dish, though.

500g soft tofu cut into 2.5cm cubes

3 tbsp vegetable oil

500g pork mince

1 large brown onion finely diced

6 cloves garlic finely chopped

1 tbsp grated ginger

1 tbsp chilli bean sauce
I use Pun Chun

1½ tbsp crispy chilli oil
I use Lao Gan Ma

1½ tbsp chilli oil I use Koon Yick

4 Thai dried chillies

½ tsp Kashmiri chilli powder

1 tbsp Shaoxing rice wine

1 tbsp white soy sauce

1 tsp dark soy sauce

2 tsp kombu extract
or 2 tsp dashi liquid at a pinch

2 tsp Chinkiang black vinegar

1 tsp soybean paste

½ tsp ground white pepper

2 tbsp canned water chestnuts sliced

500ml (2 cups) good-quality chicken stock

½ tsp sea salt

1 tsp sugar

3 tsp cornflour mixed with 2 tbsp cold water

2 spring onions cut into 2cm lengths

1 tsp ground red Sichuan peppercorns

12 slices of white bread

Butter for spreading

Bring a large saucepan of water to just below a simmer over medium heat. Add the tofu and cook for 5–10 minutes to warm through. Drain and set aside.

Meanwhile, heat 2 tbsp of the oil in a wok over high heat, then add the pork mince and saute, breaking up any larger pieces with the back of a wooden spoon, for 6–7 minutes, until well-browned. Remove from the wok and set aside.

Return the wok to medium heat and add the remaining oil. Add the onion and saute for 5–7 minutes, until translucent. Add the garlic and ginger and cook for 30–60 seconds, until aromatic, then add the chilli bean sauce, reduce the heat to medium–low and cook for 1–2 minutes, until the oil turns red. Add both types of chilli oil, the dried chillies and chilli powder and cook briefly until combined, then return the pork mince to the wok, increase the heat to medium and stir through. Deglaze the rim of the pan with the Shaoxing rice wine, then stir through both types of soy sauce, the kombu extract, black vinegar, soybean paste and white pepper. Add the drained tofu, water chestnut and chicken stock and stir to create a loose sauce consistency. Bring to a simmer while stirring gently. Taste before adjusting with salt and sugar (usually more sugar than salt to balance).

Give the cornflour slurry a quick stir, then slowly add to the mapo tofu to thicken the mixture. Wait for the sauce to boil before adding more slurry as it thickens through heat. Thicken until the sauce coats the tofu, but is not gluggy. Stir through the spring onion and ground Sichuan peppercorns, then remove from the heat.

> You'll have plenty of mapo tofu left over. Keep it in an airtight container and store in the fridge for up to three days. It makes a great dinner, even without bread.

To assemble the jaffles, place slices of white bread on a flat surface, then butter generously and turn them over, buttered side down. Cover half the bread slices with 2–3 heaped tbsp of the mapo tofu, then gently enclose with the remaining bread slices, buttered side up. Place in a jaffle maker and cook until golden and toasted to your liking.

Slices of Life

By Mike Russell,
Baker Bleu

Bread is one of the oldest foods there is and plays a role in every major culture on the planet. And yet, bakers are still discovering (or rediscovering, perhaps) ways to improve upon it. Mike Russell is one of them. At his business, Baker Bleu, he bakes some Melbourne's finest loaves. Here are six of his picks to look out for.

FOUGASSE

A decorative loaf sculpted into a pattern resembling the ear of a wheat grain, and closely associated with Provence. Often, a fougasse contains extras such as olives or anchovies. In ancient Rome, bakers made panis focacius ("hearth bread"), a flatbread baked in a hearth's ashes, leading eventually to the Italian focaccia and fougasse. It's large, round and has plenty of crispy edges, making it a great sharing bread. Enjoy with some goat's cheese or vintage cheddar. It also makes a very delicious toastie.

FICELLE

A crisp white sourdough stick. Ficelle means "string" in French and as such is skinnier and crunchier than a classic baguette. Ficelles are a great bread for a cheese board, or delicious for lunch with a smear of butter and some freshly shaved ham.

SOURDOUGH

A traditional bread-making technique that dates back to at least ancient Egypt. The bread is leavened using wild microorganisms (yeast and *lactobacillus* bacteria) rather than a commercially cultivated yeast. Sourdough, including white varieties, is naturally low GI compared to commercial bread due to the acid that *lactobacilli* (the same bacteria used to make yoghurt) produce during fermentation. And as the name suggests, there's a mild sour flavour. Delicious! The industrialisation of bread has favoured paler blond loaves. Historically, pre-industrialisation, darker loaves like this were the standard. Sourdough's complex flavour makes it ideal for eating fresh, with a smear of high-quality butter if you need it.

CIABATTA

A very new invention, introduced in 1982 by Veronese baker Arnaldo Cavallari, who was frustrated by the popularity of baguettes imported from France. He thought the loaf looked like a ciabatta ("slipper"). Made with olive oil and a very wet dough, ciabatta is a particularly moist roll, and a lighter alternative to other breads. This, and the petite shape, make it perfect for dipping into soups and sauces (olive oil especially) or making a panini.

RAISIN AND PECAN BATARD

A classic, yet lesser known, fruit and nut loaf. Excellent for cheese platters or for making John Paul Twomey's piquillo peppers, goat's cheese and pickled red onion toast (page 70).

DARK RYE

In Scandinavia you'll find vörtbröd – literally, "wort bread" – bread made from wort, the sweet malty liquid breweries make by steeping sprouted rye, barley and other grains in hot water. Once fermented, this makes beer. If stored in a cool, dry place, this wonderfully moist dark rye lasts at least a couple of weeks. The bread will reach its optimum flavour on day three. It's also a very nutritious loaf being low GI, high fibre, and rich in B vitamins, iron and magnesium. Its dark flavour profile is ideal for pairing with smoked salmon, pastrami, pickles, mustard, horseradish, cheese and avocado.

SNAPPER CEVICHE
ALEJANDRO SARAVIA, PASTUSO

Prep time 10 minutes

Cook time 20–25 minutes

Serves 8

Ceviche is the star dish of Peruvian cuisine. It's simply raw fish, lightly marinated – or cured – in citrus juice, onion and aji amarillo, a local variety of chilli. We Peruvians pride ourselves on having the best ceviche in the world, even though Mexico and some other Latin American countries have their own versions.

I come from Lima, the coastal capital, where ceviche is famous in homes and restaurants alike. For me, the dish takes me back to childhood memories of going to the fish markets with my grandmother, and selecting the fish or seafood we would be using at home.

It's a ritual. It's a dish that brings friends together for a Saturday lunch and then families on a Sunday. There will often be a table full of different ceviches. You have some little snacks and a pisco sour to start, then go on to beers, and then more pisco sours.

800g skinless snapper fillets pin-boned

250ml (1 cup) fresh orange juice

1 cinnamon quill

2 cloves

100g raw sugar

¼ sweet potato peeled and cut into 8 × 5mm rounds

LECHE DE TIGRE

½ golden shallot roughly chopped

2 raw scallops

3 coriander roots scraped and cleaned, roughly chopped, plus a handful of leaves, to serve

2 tsp aji amarillo (Peruvian yellow chilli paste) or red or green chilli deseeded and finely chopped

80ml (⅓ cup) fish stock

Sea salt

Juice of 1 lime

Juice of 2 lemons

Clean the snapper fillets and dice into 1cm cubes. Set aside ¼ cup of the offcuts, then cover the fish and set aside in the fridge.

> The quality of the fish is very important. Look for snapper with clear eyes, tender flesh, deep red gills and no fishy smell. You can't make Peruvian ceviche unless you have the freshest of fish. If you can't find snapper, look for semi-firm, white fish with flesh that doesn't flake easily.

For the leche de tigre, place the fish offcuts, shallot, scallops, coriander roots, aji amarillo and fish stock in a blender and blitz to combine. Taste and season with salt, if needed. Transfer the mixture to a bowl, stir through the lime and lemon juice and set aside in the fridge.

Heat the orange juice, cinnamon, cloves and sugar in a saucepan over medium heat and stir until the sugar has dissolved. Add the sweet potato and enough water to just cover, then cook for about 10 minutes, until tender. Drain and discard the cinnamon and cloves.

Place the fish in a shallow serving bowl. Stir the leche de tigre, then pour it over the fish and toss gently to coat. Serve with a slice of sweet potato and a couple of coriander leaves.

> The addition of sweet potato is traditional in Peruvian ceviche, its sweetness balancing the acidity of the leche de tigre. It's always served sliced, on the side.

BARBEQUED CHICKEN WINGS WITH TOUM
JOSEPH ABBOUD, RUMI

Prep time 10–15 minutes
Cook time 15–20 minutes
Serves 2–4

8 chicken wings
1 brown onion roughly chopped
25ml olive oil
2 tsp red Aleppo pepper
2 tsp black Aleppo pepper
1 tsp ground sumac

TOUM
25g garlic cloves peeled
Pinch of sea salt
125ml (½ cup) vegetable oil
2 tsp lemon juice

When I was growing up, everything cooked on the barbeque was intentionally a bit charred. After we'd finished eating, Mum would always bring out the eggplants and put them straight over the coals to make baba ganoush. Lebanese people do the best eggplant in the world, I reckon, and charring really brings out their bittersweet flavour.

When I worked at Est Est Est and other fine-dining restaurants, everything had to be this beautiful golden-brown. I remember barbequing some wings like that for my family and everyone said, "Can you put these back on? They're not cooked." It was so funny.

When we opened Rumi, we had a little $60 charcoal barbeque that we bought at a Middle Eastern shop, and we used that for the first 10 years. There was never any question about whether we might use a gas one – I think the gas ones are ridiculous.

At Rumi we always marinate our meats in onion juice, which is an Iranian method. It tenderises the meat and adds a bit of sweetness. The sumac adds a nice sour finish and a powdery, lip-coating texture.

To make the toum, pound the garlic, salt and 2 tsp of the oil to a smooth paste using a large mortar and pestle. Add half the lemon juice and stir to combine, then very, very slowly add the remaining oil in a slow, steady stream, pausing to add a few drops of lemon juice now and then, until the toum is firm and emulsified.

> The toum recipe makes more than you will need here. It will keep in an airtight container in the fridge for 5–7 days. You can put toum on bloody everything. People freak out when they realise it's just raw garlic, salt and lemon. It just comes together like magic.

Separate the wingettes and drummettes by cutting through the chicken wing joints with a sharp knife, then remove the wing tips and discard. Set aside in a large bowl.

Blitz the onion in a food processor until finely chopped, then strain through a fine-meshed sieve lined with a clean Chux cloth into a bowl. Gently squeeze the cloth to extract the juice from the onion. Add 25ml of the onion juice and the olive oil to the chicken wings and massage to coat.

> For freshness, I use Aussie olive oil – a lot of the stuff that comes from overseas is already getting on and past its best.

→

"I prefer regular eggplants, which have way more flesh. I actually don't like Lebanese eggplants!"

Snacks & Starters

Barbequed chicken wings with toum continued

Skewer the wings, alternating the wingettes and drumettes, then refrigerate, uncovered, until required. (You can skip the skewers if you don't have any to hand.)

Preheat a charcoal barbeque to medium–hot. Once the flames have died down and the coals have a dusting of white ash, add the chicken skewers and cook, turning occasionally, for 15–20 minutes, until cooked through and the skin is golden and crisp – a little char on the wings is fine.

Transfer the chicken to a serving dish and generously brush with some of the toum. Sprinkle with the Aleppo peppers and sumac, and serve.

> Look for Aleppo pepper at Middle Eastern grocers. I buy mine from the Brunswick Market on Sydney Road.

BABA GANOUSH
JOSEPH ABBOUD, RUMI

Prep time 5–10 minutes

Cook time 20 minutes, plus 15 minutes cooling

Serves 4

2 large eggplants

2 cloves garlic

Sea salt

1 tbsp olive oil plus extra for drizzling

3 tbsp tahini

Juice of 1 lemon

¼ tsp nigella seeds

Preheat a charcoal or gas barbeque to high.

Trim the green tops off the eggplants and prick all over with a knife, then place on the barbeque and cook, turning frequently, for 15–20 minutes, until the skins have blackened and the eggplant is very soft.

Transfer the eggplant to a colander to drain and set aside for about 15 minutes or until cool enough to handle. Remove the blackened skins and place the caramelised eggplant flesh in a bowl.

Place the garlic and a pinch of salt in a mortar and crush with the pestle to a fine paste. Transfer the garlic to the bowl with the eggplant and add the olive oil, tahini and lemon juice. Whisk the ingredients together to help break up the eggplant and achieve a chunky finish.

> Look for Al Kanater tahini, which comes from Lebanon but is widely available here. When you open the bucket it smells beautiful and roasty.

Transfer the baba ganoush to a plate or bowl. Make a well in the centre using the back of a spoon and drizzle with a little extra olive oil. Sprinkle with the nigella seeds and serve with your favourite bread.

See page 40 for an image of the dish.

ZUCCHINI DUMPLINGS
YING HOU AND MEIYAN WANG, SHANDONG MAMA

Prep time 15 minutes, plus 45 minutes if making your own dumpling wrappers

Cook time 5–10 minutes

Makes 24

At Shandong Mama, we were initially known for our mackerel dumplings, until one day we reviewed our sales records and noticed the vegan zucchini dumplings had risen from the bottom of the list to become our bestselling item. The recipe isn't particularly hard or complicated, but our customers' enthusiasm for these dumplings felt like a sign our hard work was being recognised and appreciated.

These dumplings have a slightly thicker skin to prevent them from breaking open as they boil. Unlike other dumpling fillings, the air in the mixture expands like a small balloon. When training new staff members we always put one or two extra dumplings in the saucepan, as they can break easily if not watched closely.

In many recipes, the flavour of zucchini is overpowered by other ingredients, but when Mama created these dumplings, she used oil to add richness, retaining as much of the zucchini's taste and texture as possible.

Choose small- to medium-sized zucchini that feel heavy for their size. The larger ones are usually watery and have larger seeds. If you can still see the fine hair on the skin, that means they're very fresh.

Making dumplings is great fun and should be a social occasion. In Chinese families, fathers and uncles usually sit quietly rolling the dumpling wrappers at one corner of the kitchen bench, while the mums and aunties sit around the mixing bowl, wrapping the dumplings with professional speed and chatting about all that's happened lately. If you sit near them for an hour, you won't miss a thing about their lives.

500g zucchini

1 tsp sea salt

60g tofu puffs cut into 5mm cubes

2–3 spring onions white part only, finely chopped

½ bunch coriander finely chopped

½ tsp shiitake mushroom powder

1½ tbsp peanut oil

5 tsp sesame oil

DUMPLING WRAPPERS

250g high protein wheat flour plus extra for dusting

1 tsp sea salt

OR 24 store-bought dumpling wrappers

Grate the zucchini using the large holes of a box grater, then transfer to a bowl and toss through the salt until evenly combined. Set aside for 20 minutes, then place the zucchini in a clean tea towel, gather up the sides and squeeze out all the juice. When you open the tea towel the zucchini should remain in a ball – if it falls apart then the zucchini is still too wet and you'll need to squeeze again.

Roughly chop the zucchini, then place in a large bowl with the tofu puffs, spring onion and coriander. Add the shiitake powder, peanut oil and sesame oil and toss everything together until well combined. Check the seasoning, then set aside.

If you want to make your own dumpling wrappers, place the flour in the bowl of a stand mixer with the dough hook attached. Dissolve the salt in 125ml (½ cup) of water, then slowly add to the flour, while mixing on low speed. Increase the speed to medium and knead for 10 minutes or until smooth.

Place the dough in a bowl, cover with a tea towel and let it rest for 30 minutes.
→

Zucchini dumplings continued

Briefly knead the dough for 2–3 minutes, then roll it into a baguette shape. Cut into 24 even pieces, each weighing 14g, then dust generously in flour.

Roll the dough portions into 9–10cm circles, trying to keep the wrappers thinner at the edge and thicker in the middle (this prevents the dumpling filling soaking though the base of the dumplings). Stack the wrappers as you go and keep them covered with a clean tea towel to stop them drying out.

This is the fun part. To assemble the dumplings, place 1 scant tbsp of filling in the middle of each dumpling wrapper, then fold the wrapper over the filling and gently press the edges together at the top to seal. Press the outer edges of the dumpling together, then work your way towards the middle until the filling is completely sealed. Your first dumpling is done, now repeat with the remaining filling and dumpling wrappers.

Bring a large saucepan of water to the boil over medium heat and add the dumplings. When the water returns to the boil, add 125ml (½ cup) of water. Repeat this step 2–3 times, until the dumpling edges are translucent – this should take about 4.5 minutes.

Drain and transfer to a serving plate. Serve with your choice of dipping sauce. Enjoy.

STRACCIATELLA, WALNUT AND CIME DI RAPA
DAVID VERHEUL, EMBLA

Prep time 10–12 minutes

Cook time about 15 minutes

Serves 4–6

Most of the food at Embla is Italian, it's just not presented in a way that is classically Italian. In this recipe, for example, the way the cime di rapa is broken down in olive oil is old Italian nonna stuff. (I think I probably was an old Italian nonna in a previous life.) Cime di rapa, a bitter green a bit like kale, is a classic Italian ingredient in itself. This technique smooths out the bitterness a bit, but it's still quite pungent, iron-y and a little bit sulphurous. Paired with the creamy stracciatella, which rounds everything out, and the walnut pesto, which brings texture and nuttiness, it all comes together nicely.

Most store-bought walnuts are extremely old and stale. Find some walnuts that haven't been in a cool store for a couple of years – ideally, buy them directly from a grower at a farmers' market. This will completely change what you think about walnuts, in my opinion. At Embla we buy walnuts from Mike at Otway Walnuts. He's incredibly passionate and his nuts are bloody fantastic.

1 bunch cime di rapa

2 tbsp oregano leaves

2 cloves garlic finely sliced

½ tsp chilli flakes

100ml olive oil

Sea salt and freshly ground black pepper

200g stracciatella

Crackers to serve

WALNUT PESTO

100g walnuts roughly chopped

1 clove garlic finely chopped

20g finely grated parmesan

100ml olive oil

Sea salt and freshly ground black pepper

Remove the leaves and florets from the cime di rapa and set aside in a large frying pan. Lightly peel the stalks if they look particularly woody and fibrous, then slice into 1cm thick pieces and add to the pan, along with the oregano, garlic, chilli flakes and olive oil.

Place the pan over medium heat and cook for 12–15 minutes, until the leaves and florets are wilted. Season with salt and pepper, then remove from the heat and set aside to cool.

To make the walnut pesto, simply combine the ingredients in a bowl and season to taste.

To serve, scoop the stracciatella into a shallow serving dish, then place the cime di rapa and walnut pesto beside it, so it looks like a savoury Neapolitan ice cream. Serve with your favourite crackers.

"Read the entire recipe through before you start. That was a great tip given to me as a child. If you don't read the entire recipe through first, you might miss a step."

KARAAGE CHICKEN RIBS
JARROD DI BLASI, IZAKAYA DEN 2029

Prep time 10 minutes, plus
3 hours 30 minutes marinating

Cook time 25 minutes

Serves 4

Izakaya Den was my favourite restaurant for 10 years. So even before I started working there as head chef, my heart was there already. This dish has been on the menu since day one and it's something I've ordered myself many times.

When we refreshed the restaurant in 2020, we thought it would be a nice homage to keep the chicken. I tweaked it slightly, so it's kind of a reincarnation – which is why we call it Den Chicken 2.0 on the menu. It sounds crazy, but I don't think I've ever spent more time on one dish in my whole career.

With this particular recipe, we noticed something really interesting: the marinade on the chicken is so strong that it seasons the oil. So, if you're having a dinner party and you're like, "Alright, I'm gonna do this chicken recipe!" a great trick is to get the oil out several hours before you plan on cooking, and fry a few pieces. Then, when you reheat the oil to cook the rest of the chicken, it just tastes better. It's more flavoursome and well rounded.

See page 55 for an image of the dish.

180ml soy sauce

25ml sake

1 tsp finely grated ginger

1 tsp finely chopped garlic

1 tsp hot English mustard

1 tbsp curry powder we use S&B

1kg chicken ribs

500g potato starch we use Tung Chun

2L vegetable oil for deep-frying

Kewpie mayonnaise to serve

Place the soy sauce, sake, ginger, garlic, mustard and curry powder in a large bowl and whisk until well combined. Add the chicken ribs and stir to completely coat in the marinade. Cover and set aside in the fridge for 1.5 hours.

Place the potato starch on a large plate. Working with one piece at a time, toss the ribs in the potato starch, pressing down to completely coat both sides evenly. Layer the ribs on top of each other in an airtight container and set aside in the fridge for at least 2 hours.

> When you layer each piece on top of each other in the right container, you get the marinated chicken and the potato starch sitting on top of each other. The chicken starts to absorb the potato starch and the end product is crunchy, golden and amazing.

Heat the oil in a large saucepan to 160°C on a kitchen thermometer. Place a maximum of four ribs in the pan and cook for 6 minutes until crisp and golden brown. Transfer to a plate lined with paper towel to drain while you cook the remaining ribs.

> It's hard to overcook chicken, but for juiciness and texture we've found that 6 minutes of fry time is absolutely optimal. And we've tried it minute-by-minute, every which way.

Place the fried chicken ribs neatly onto a serving plate and serve with Kewpie mayonnaise on the side.

Snacks & Starters

EBI TOAST
CAELAN O'ROURKE, RAPHAEL HYAMS AND GEOFF MARETT, NAMA

Prep time 20 minutes
Cook time 30 minutes
Serves 4–6

This dish – which combines prawn mousse, umami-packed "Namamite" and caviar – is the result of a drunken 2am conversation about wanting to create a version of the yum cha staple, prawn toast.

The Namamite was conceived earlier for another dish (which was then completely forgotten about, because once the Namamite found its way onto ebi toast, life was never quite the same). It was inspired by the similarity in smell between shio kombu (salted kelp) and Vegemite. We became obsessed with the idea of making a Japanese-inspired Vegemite and it all spiralled from there.

Finally: in 2020 we worked closely with the gentleman at Yarra Valley Caviar. As we tended the ponds and milked caviar from the fish, we had what alcoholics refer to as a "moment of clarity" and decided that caviar must be heaped on top of the Namamite. We are indulgent people and this is most certainly an indulgent dish!

See page 54 for an image of the dish.

400g Turkish bread
500g raw peeled frozen **prawns** thawed
2 egg whites
1 tsp hondashi powder
150g nama panko breadcrumbs fresh Japanese breadcrumbs
Vegetable oil for deep-frying
Snipped chives to serve
Sesame seeds to serve
Yarra Valley Caviar to serve (optional)

NAMAMITE
50g shio kombu
30ml tamari or soy sauce
30ml Chinkiang black vinegar
1 tbsp nori paste
2 tsp hot water

To make the "Namamite", pop the ingredients in a tall jug and use a stick blender to blitz until thick, but still a little loose. As the mixture cools, the natural gelatine in the nori will solidify, leaving you with a paste that looks glossier and slightly looser than vegemite. In short, it should be easily spreadable.

Slice the Turkish bread into 16 pieces, about 2cm wide.

In the bowl of a food processor, blitz the prawns, egg whites and hondashi powder to a smooth consistency, then evenly spoon the mixture onto the cut sides of the Turkish bread.

Place the breadcrumbs on a large plate, then press the Turkish bread, prawn side down, into the breadcrumbs until evenly coated.

Heat enough vegetable oil for deep-frying in a large saucepan to 180°C on a kitchen thermometer. Working in batches, add the ebi toast and cook for 3–4 minutes, turning halfway through cooking, until nice and crispy. Using a slotted spoon, transfer to a wire rack with paper towel underneath to drain.

Gently brush the Namamite over the top of each ebi toast (use sparingly as it's very rich), then sprinkle with chives, sesame seeds and caviar (if using).

Cut the ebi toasts in half and serve immediately.

The left-over Namamite will keep in an airtight container in the fridge for up to 1 month.

"The caviar is a boujie addition that isn't 100 per cent necessary if you don't want to break the bank."

Left: Ebi toast, page 53; Right: Karaage chicken ribs, page 52

"S&B is a really famous brand of curry powder. The powder itself is mild and aromatic and really different to what you'd usually associate with curry powder, and has that specific Japanese curry flavour."

WHAT CHEFS HAVE READY WHEN FRIENDS ARRIVE

HUGH ALLEN, VUE DE MONDE

Champagne popped open with a sabre (sword). It started off as a bit of a joke at work, but now we always do it when we're having drinks at someone's house, without thinking about it. We just use the back of a bread knife. I like Ulysse Collin.

ANDREAS PAPADAKIS, OSTERIA ILARIA

I love champagne. You can drink a nice one – like Larmandier-Bernier – all evening. Yes, it's expensive, but it's always consistent, always amazing and actually goes with most meals.

SHANE DELIA, MAHA

I'm always a gin and tonic guy, just because it's nice and clean and easy to put together. At the moment I really like Four Pillars' Olive Leaf Gin. But I've always got bottles of champagne in the fridge. The path of least resistance is the one that I like – something nice and quick.

CHAVALIT PIYAPHANEE, SOI 38

I'm a gin man. I have it straight with ice, or with tonic if someone doesn't like it neat. It's refreshing and complements Thai food – all spicy food, actually – really well.

VICTOR LIONG, LEE HO FOOK

I'm a huge fan of a super cold gin Martini. Here's a tip: pre-batch them, and pour them from the freezer directly into frozen glasses. When it comes to Martinis, the colder the better. The freezer Martini is dangerous, though, because it's too easy to say, "I've had a hard day," then later wonder why you're suddenly quite so happy, and it's because you've had three Martinis.

SHANNON MARTINEZ, SMITH & DAUGHTERS

I generally like to start the party off with shots of tequila, just because that gets everyone in the mood. Then maybe a gin-based cocktail, like a White Lady or something. They're pretty nice. Then move onto wine, and then back into the shots.

MATT LANE, MAMASITA

A classic Margarita shaken up with tequila, Cointreau, agave syrup and lime, then poured over ice into a tumbler. It loosens the lips and reduces social anxiety among the group quickly. But if it's a daytime thing, an Aperol spritz or another spritz. They're a bit lower alcohol; not as intense. You can drink a few and they don't knock you for a six. And for guys and girls alike, everyone enjoys a spritz.

JESSE GERNER, BOMBA

Manzanilla, which is a really light sherry. It's quite minerally and works well with cheeses and oysters. It's a great kick off. At home, I do this play on the original idea of tapas: I pre-pour all the glasses of manzanilla, then put a slice of bread with some jamon or cheese on top of each one. So if you have a dozen people coming over, you can have it all set up on arrival so everyone gets a bite to eat right away. And if it's a hot day and there are flies around, the bread keeps them out of the glasses. Look for La Goya manzanilla, which is easy to find.

DAVE VERHEUL, EMBLA

I'm a bitter drink nerd. I actually have my own vermouth label – Saison Vermouth. So it's vermouth on ice, with a wedge of citrus. It's sweet, bitter and the ABV isn't too high. And you can chuck a bit of soda or tonic in there and make it even lighter again. It's an aperitivo for a reason – it's there to whet your palate and make you hungry.

JOEY KELLOCK, 1800 LASAGNE

It's funny, I don't have people over very much, but when I do I'm a sucker for a Negroni. It knocks a good solid edge off in one go. It just tastes so good, and it's so simple and so nostalgic – it's filled with so much feeling. It's just the king of cocktails, the king of mixed magic.

ALMAY JORDAAN, OLD PALM LIQUOR

I'm plain, simple and very much inspired by Elizabeth David's book *An Omelette and a Glass of Wine* when it comes to eating and entertaining. But I have my husband Simon, who is literally my personal sommelier. The last wine I really enjoyed was Anne et Jean-Francois Ganevat Chardonnay, from the Jura in France. I don't like typical chardonnays, which are big, buttery and heavy. This one is really different.

"You can, of course,
add pork liver pate.
I get mine from City Larder.
It's my go-to."

BANH MI
THI LE, ANCHOVY

Prep time 1 hour 15 minutes,
plus overnight soaking

Cook time about 10 minutes

Serves 4

This banh mi was born from COVID – it's a lockdown recipe. During that time, we stopped doing Anchovy's food and instead created a Laotian-inspired takeaway menu. I just wanted to cook food that I liked eating.

We were making lots of Laotian-style herbal sausages at the time, so we decided to do the Lao version of banh mi: khao jee pate. We figured that people were more familiar with the name banh mi, so that's what we decided to call it, to get people to try it. Normally a banh mi would have pate, but we left it out as we didn't want it to hide all the effort we put into making the sausage. For home, we recommend rolling the sausage mix into meatballs.

The bread is crucial to a good banh mi. You can't go fancy and use sourdough; it needs to be that Vietnamese-style super-light, very crusty and crunchy roll and it needs to be fresh – it's all about the texture. The bread is there as a vessel, it shouldn't detract from the filling. At the end of the day, what you put in a banh mi is entirely up to you. Play around until you've got something you're happy with.

1½ tbsp vegetable oil

4 banh mi rolls

Whole-egg mayonnaise for spreading

2 Lebanese cucumbers sliced length-ways into 8 slices, 3mm thick

4 spring onions white part only

Coriander sprigs to serve

Maggi seasoning to serve

Chilli oil to serve

PICKLED CARROT AND DAIKON

150ml rice wine vinegar

75g caster sugar

1 tsp sea salt flakes

Pinch of freshly ground black pepper

100g carrot julienned

100g daikon julienned

→

To make the pickled carrot and daikon, place the rice wine vinegar, sugar, salt and pepper in a small saucepan over low heat and bring to the boil, stirring until the sugar is dissolved.

Place the carrot and daikon in a heatproof bowl and pour the hot pickling liquid over the top, ensuring that the vegetables are submerged. Set aside to cool, then place in the fridge until ready to serve.

To make the red chilli paste, wrap the shrimp paste in foil, then place in a dry frying pan with the drained chillies, coriander seeds, cumin seeds and white peppercorns and toast over medium–high heat for 1–2 minutes, until fragrant.

Transfer the toasted spices to a mortar and pound to a fine powder with the pestle, then pound in the remaining ingredients, adding up to 1½ tbsp of water to help loosen the paste, in the following order: lemongrass, lime leaf, shallot, garlic, coriander stalks and chilli. Finally, unwrap the shrimp paste and pound that in, too, until you have a smooth, thick paste. Alternatively, you can blitz the ingredients in a blender. Transfer to a bowl and set aside.

> If you're doing this in small batches, use a mortar and pestle, which I find gives best results. For a big batch, you can use a blender. I choose to use uncooked red chilli paste because it adds a little depth to the chilli flavour. Left-over red chilli paste will keep in an airtight container in the fridge for up to 2 weeks.

→

"If I'm not making my own chilli oil, Lao Gan Ma brand is my definite go-to, or you can always swing by Anchovy and pick up a jar of our home-made stuff."

RED CHILLI PASTE

20g shrimp paste

40–50g large dried guajillo chilllies soaked in hot water overnight, drained

¼ tsp coriander seeds

¼ tsp cumin seeds

¼ tsp white peppercorns

2 lemongrass stalks white part only, finely chopped

1 large makrut lime leaf stem removed, finely chopped

1 shallot finely chopped

1 clove garlic finely chopped

25g coriander stalks finely chopped

4 bird's eye chillies finely chopped

HERB MEATBALLS

4 coriander roots scraped clean and chopped

4 makrut lime leaves roughly torn

2 bird's eye chillies roughly chopped

2 cloves garlic peeled

1 lemongrass stalk white part only, roughly chopped

1 spring onion white part only, finely sliced

½ shallot peeled and roughly chopped

6cm piece of galangal peeled and finely chopped

400g pork mince

35g (¼ cup) cooked sticky or jasmine rice

2 tsp fish sauce

⅔ tsp sugar

⅔ tsp sea salt flakes

⅓ tsp freshly ground black pepper

Banh mi continued

To make the herb meatballs, place the coriander root, lime leaves, chilli, garlic, lemongrass, spring onion, shallot and galangal in a food processor and blitz until very finely chopped. Add the pork, rice, fish sauce, sugar, salt and pepper and blitz until very well combined. Transfer to a bowl and divide the mixture into 16 meatballs.

Heat half the oil in a frying pan over medium–high heat, add eight meatballs and cook, stirring, for 5–6 minutes, until cooked through. Set aside on a plate and repeat with the remaining oil and meatballs.

To assemble your banh mi, slice the rolls open lengthways but don't cut all the way through. Spread mayonnaise on one side and a little red chilli paste on the other side. Divide the carrot and daikon pickles, cucumber, spring onion and coriander sprigs among the rolls, then stuff four meatballs into each roll. Drizzle over Maggi seasoning and a little chilli oil and serve.

If I had to choose my top two bakeries in Melbourne, it would probably be Phuoc Thanh on Victoria Street in Richmond and Nhu Lan on Hopkins Street in Footscray.

DRUNKEN PIPIS WITH ROLLED RICE NOODLES AND GINGER CHICKEN FAT
VICTOR LIONG, LEE HO FOOK

Prep time 10 minutes

Cook time 1 hour 30 minutes

Serves 4

I love making this dish because it's easy, and that's important when you're cooking at home. I also love it because I grew up in Southern China, and the drunken technique is more typical of Shanghai in the north, so I discovered it quite late. For me, those drunken, smoked, northern flavour profiles are still exciting.

Drunken, which is when you poach or marinate meats or seafood in an alcohol such as rice wine, is a great technique. This preparation highlights the fresh shellfish flavours, which marry with the fragrant rice wine for a savoury freshness you most often find in coastal Chinese cuisines, from Shanghai to Canton.

Slippery rice noodles and luscious ginger chicken fat make this an amazing hot starter in the colder months. For summer, you can forego the noodles and fat, keep the pipis marinating for longer and serve the dish cold. It's a nice way to eat pipis that isn't just XO sauce – I like the versatility of it, and it's wine-friendly, too.

500g pipis rinsed and drained (we use Goolwa pipis)

Large pinch of ground white pepper

200g rolled rice noodles also known as cheong fun, cut into 2cm lengths

1 bunch flowering garlic chives cut into 3cm lengths

GINGER CHICKEN FAT

500g chicken skin ask your butcher for this

6cm piece of ginger peeled and sliced

2 spring onions white part only, cut into 4cm lengths

DRUNKEN SAUCE

2 tbsp sugar

3 tsp white soy sauce or tamari

3 tbsp aged Shaoxing rice wine

To make the ginger chicken fat, place the chicken skin in a frying pan and cover with 500ml (2 cups) of water. Gently bring to the boil over medium heat and cook for 7–8 minutes, then reduce the heat to a simmer and cook, stirring occasionally to stop the skins sticking together and burning, for about 50 minutes, until the fat has rendered and the water has evaporated. At this stage the skin will slowly start deep-frying in its own fat and turn golden brown. Add the ginger and spring onion and cook for 10 minutes, until aromatic, then remove from the heat and strain the fat through a fine-meshed sieve into a bowl. Discard the solids.

Meanwhile, to make the drunken sauce, combine the ingredients and 2 tbsp of water in a small bowl and stir to combine.

Place 200ml of water in a wide shallow saucepan and bring to the boil over high heat. Add the pipis, then cover and allow them to steam for 1–2 minutes, until they open. Using a slotted spoon, transfer the pipis to a plate. Add 30–50ml of the drunken sauce to the pan, along with the white pepper, and stir to combine. The taste should be intensely fragrant from the rice wine as well as briny and savoury and with a gentle warmth from the pepper. Stir the pipis back into the sauce and keep warm.

Cook the noodles according to the packet instructions, then place in the bottom of a serving dish. Ladle over the pipis, reserving the sauce in the pan. Gently heat the sauce over low heat, then add the garlic chives and briefly cook until they turn bright green. Spoon the sauce over the pipis and noodles and liberally drizzle with about 60ml of warm chicken fat, or more, to taste. Serve immediately.

Snacks & Starters

"At Asian grocers all the rice wines look the same and cost around $2 or $3.50 a bottle. Then there will be one bottle that's $11. Get that one. The more expensive rice wines have a deep amber colour and a grassy sweetness similar to amontillado sherry or aged sake."

"Taste everything. You should be trying as you go and adjusting the seasoning (salt). And at the end don't be afraid to add a bit of fattiness with olive oil, or acidity with lemon juice or something else. It's about finding that balance so the dish is peaking as you serve it."

SWEETCORN AND ESPELETTE MADELEINES WITH BLUE SWIMMER CRAB
NICK DELIGIANNIS, FRÉDÉRIC

Prep time 20 minutes,
plus 20 minutes resting
Cook time 25 minutes
Serves 4–6

I love this dish because it's a modern take on an iconic French classic. Madeleines are little cakes often flavoured with honey and served with custard. They're quite eye-catching due to their unique scallop-shell shape.

The inspiration for this savoury version came from my time working at Pollen Street Social in London, where we used to make corn crumpets. I always loved their texture and flavour, but thought they would be great with some spice – so I added Espelette pepper, which comes uniquely from the Basque region in France.

These make a great canape and are a definite crowd pleaser. They're sweet and savoury, but not too rich, and pair nicely with a glass of chardonnay or other white wine. This is a foolproof recipe, but it is important not to beat the batter too hard – you need to keep the air in it.

Canola oil spray
250g cooked blue swimmer crabmeat
100g canned sweetcorn drained
3 tbsp aioli
1 tsp chopped chives
Salt flakes to taste
Pinch of Espelette pepper
Zest and juice of ½ lemon

MADELEINES
4 eggs
100g caster sugar
200g (1⅓ cups) self-raising flour
1½ tsp sea salt
½ tsp baking powder
225g canned sweetcorn chopped
150ml extra-virgin olive oil
1 tsp Espelette pepper

To make the madeleines, place the eggs and caster sugar in a stand mixer with the whisk attachment and whisk on high speed for 5 minutes or until the mixture triples in volume and leaves a ribbon when the whisk is lifted (this is called a cold sabayon).

Meanwhile, double sift the flour, salt and baking powder into a large bowl. In a separate bowl, combine the chopped corn and oil and set aside.

Using a spatula, scrape the sabayon into a large bowl, then gently fold through the flour mixture, along with the Espelette pepper, keeping as much air in the mixture as possible. Once all the flour is incorporated, add the corn and oil mixture and continue to mix (the oil will make the mixture split, but it will come together after about 30 seconds). Cover with plastic wrap and allow to rest in the fridge for at least 1 hour (or even better overnight).

Preheat the oven to 180°C (fan-forced).

Place a 12-hole madeleine tray in the oven for 5 minutes to heat up, then remove and spray the holes with canola oil. Place 1 heaped tbsp of the sweetcorn batter in each of the holes (or use a piping bag), then return to the oven and bake for 12 minutes or until golden brown and the madeleines have formed a "nipple" on top. Remove from the tray and set aside to cool on a wire rack, then repeat with the remaining mixture.

Squeeze out any excess liquid from the crabmeat, then place in a bowl and add the remaining ingredients – try not to overmix the crab as you want it to be quite textural.

To serve, warm the madeleines in a 160°C oven (unless you are serving them straight away) for about 1 minute, until soft and heated through. Top with the cold crab mixture and enjoy.

Snacks & Starters

"You'll need a 12-hole madeleine tray for this recipe. You can use a muffin tray at a pinch, but the holes need to be shallow, and you won't get the distinct scallop-shell shape."

PIQUILLO PEPPERS ON TOAST
JOHN PAUL TWOMEY, BAKER BLEU

Prep time 10 minutes
Cook time 15 minutes
Serves 4

This is an easy pre-dinner snack that comes together in minutes, using items you might already have in your fridge.

On Sundays, Baker Bleu bakes a special raisin and pecan loaf, and it's perfect for this dish. The sweetness of the raisins contrasts subtly with the other savoury elements. Piquillo, a very mild Spanish pepper, adds a slight bite, while the goat's cheese brings a salty tang. It's a perfectly balanced aperitivo to start your meal.

See page 72 for an image of the dish.

---

2 slices raisin and pecan batard
or another fruit bread
2 cubes goat's feta I like Meredith Dairy
2 roasted piquillo peppers cut in half
Salt flakes and freshly ground
black pepper

PICKLED RED ONION
300g sugar
600g white wine vinegar
1 cinnamon quill
2 cloves
1 star anise
2 red onions quartered

To make the pickled red onion, place the sugar, vinegar and spices in a small saucepan and bring to a simmer over medium heat. Add the onion and allow the mixture to return to a simmer, then remove from the heat. Set aside until cool.

Toast the bread, then spread a cube of goat's feta over of each slice. Slice the toast in half, then top each slice with the piquillo pepper and a few slices of pickled red onion. Season with salt and pepper and serve.

JAMON AND LEEK CROQUETAS
ERNEST TOVAR, NÓMADA

Prep time 20–25 minutes, plus 1 hour chilling

Cook time 30–55 minutes

Serves 4–6

I'm not sure I can really call this recipe mine. It's very classic and representative of the jamon and leek croquetas you find in tapas bars, takeaway delis and homes all over Spain – from my hometown of Barcelona, to Seville in the south. Salted cod croquetas and manchego croquetas are two others that are really popular and well worth a try.

Unlike French croquettes, you won't find any potato in true Spanish croquetas. We call those bombas, and they're filled with mashed potato and some sort of meat, like chorizo or beef.

I'm yet to meet someone who doesn't love a classic jamon croqueta, and once you tackle this recipe you'll see how simple they are.

See page 72 for an image of the dish.

150g unsalted butter

750ml (3 cups) full-cream milk

Sea salt and freshly ground black pepper

½ leek white part only, finely sliced

300g (2 cups) plain flour

125g jamon serrano finely diced

4 eggs lightly beaten

250g panko breadcrumbs

1L vegetable oil for deep-frying

Salt flakes to serve

Place two saucepans over medium heat. Melt the butter in one pan and slowly heat the milk in the other pan to just below boiling. Season the milk with a pinch of salt and pepper.

Meanwhile, add the leek to the melted butter, reduce the heat to low and cook for about 10 minutes, until soft and translucent, but not browned. Add half the flour and stir vigorously to combine, ensuring there are no lumps. Increase the heat to medium–high and cook for 3–4 minutes, stirring constantly. You want to cook out the floury taste, without burning the roux on the base of the pan (feel free to taste the roux to ensure it isn't floury). Reduce the heat to low, then add the jamon and stir through for 1–2 minutes, to allow the jamon to release some of its delicious fat through the roux.

Increase the heat to medium, pour the hot milk into the pan and stir vigorously for about 5 minutes or until the mixture is very thick and no lumps remain. You will know it is ready when the mixture starts to pull away from the side of the pan and has a slightly shiny appearance.

> To make a simple vegetarian croqueta, substitute the jamon for 150g grated manchego, adding it just before you remove the croqueta mixture from the heat.

Spoon the mixture in an even layer onto a baking tray lined with baking paper, then cover with another piece of baking paper to prevent a skin forming. Set aside to cool to room temperature, then place in the fridge for 1 hour.

→

"The pickled red onion recipe makes more than you need here, but it will keep in an airtight container in the fridge for up to 2 months."

Jamon and leek croquetas continued

Divide the croqueta mixture into 50g portions, then shape each portion into a log the same diameter as a 20-cent coin. Return to the fridge while you prepare a crumbing station.

To crumb the croquetas, grab three shallow bowls. Place the remaining flour in one bowl, the beaten egg in another and the breadcrumbs in the third.

Take two or three croquetas (no more) and toss them through the flour. Give them a shake to remove any excess flour, then roll in the egg to completely coat. Shake again to remove the excess, then transfer to the breadcrumbs and give the croquetas another good roll around. It doesn't hurt to give them a gentle squeeze at this stage to help the crumb stick and reform their shape. Repeat this process to make about 20 croquetas. (Pro tip: the more flour, egg and breadcrumbs you use, the easier it is to achieve perfectly crumbed croquetas.) Place the crumbed croquetas in the fridge.

Heat the vegetable oil in a large heavy-based saucepan to 180°C on a kitchen thermometer.

Gently cook three or four croquetas at a time for about 3 minutes, gently turning with a slotted spoon, until golden brown. Transfer to a plate lined with paper towel to drain, then serve, sprinkled with salt flakes.

ELOTES (STREET-STYLE GRILLED CORN)
MATT LANE, MAMASITA

Prep time 5 minutes

Cook time 15 minutes

Serves 4

Elotes is the Spanish word for corn, but in Mexico it tends to refer to a particular street snack: grilled corn on the cob topped with mayo, grated cheese, chilli and lime. It's easy to make and my kids love it, though they eat it with plain mayo rather than the chipotle-spiked version here. Store-bought mayo is fine if you don't want to make your own – simply stir through the chipotle in adobo sauce before serving.

4 sweetcorn cobs husked and halved crossways

100–125g cotija or parmesan finely grated

1 lime quartered

CHIPOTLE MAYONNAISE

2 egg yolks

Juice of 1½ large limes

1½ tsp cider vinegar

200ml light olive oil

20g chipotle in adobo sauce finely chopped

Sea salt

Bring a large saucepan of water to the boil over high heat. Add the corn and cook for 5 minutes or until tender. Drain and set aside.

Meanwhile, to make the chipotle mayonnaise, whisk the egg yolks, lime juice and cider vinegar in a bowl. Very slowly, start adding the oil a few drops at a time while continually whisking, then continue to add the oil in a slow, steady stream until you have an emulsified, smooth mayonnaise (add a little warm water if it's getting too thick). Stir in the chipotle and season with salt to taste.

Heat a lightly oiled barbeque grill to high or a griddle pan over high heat. Add the corn and cook for 10–12 minutes, until nicely charred on all sides. (I often don't bother with this step at home.)

Brush the corn with the chipotle mayo (or plain mayo for kids), then sprinkle with the cheese, add a squeeze of lime and eat.

Any left-over chipotle mayo will keep in the fridge for 5–7 days.

"For the full experience, enjoy with a pot of premium oolong tea."

PORK AND PRAWN SIU MAI
DAVID ZHOU, DAVID'S AND ORIENTAL TEAHOUSE

Prep time 1 hour
Cook time 15 minutes
Makes 35

I remember the first time I ever ate siu mai. It was in Shanghai, where I grew up, at this trendy yum cha restaurant that had just opened. I had it for breakfast at around 6am and it was so fresh. What a great way to start the day. Afterwards, I took my girlfriend there for us to enjoy it together. That girlfriend later became my wife, and to this day we still remember the round table where we sat, the aromas of that restaurant and the pork and prawn siu mai.

This Cantonese-style recipe is inspired by those same siu mai. The filling is a pork and prawn mixture that is slightly bouncy and delicate at the same time. Decades later, I still have the same morning ritual here in Melbourne. An early start, time spent with my wife over a few servings of quality fresh dumplings and a good pot of oolong tea.

30g dried shiitake mushrooms

600g minced pork

2½ tsp cornflour

1 tsp sea salt

250g peeled raw prawns finely chopped

2½ tsp sugar

2 tsp light soy sauce

2 tsp oyster sauce

1½ tbsp vegetable oil

35 round wonton wrappers

¼ red capsicum very finely diced

1 tsp Lao Gan Ma Crispy Chilli Oil get the chilli pieces and oil, plus extra oil to taste

SOY AND CHILLI DIPPING SAUCE

50ml light soy sauce

2 tsp sugar

1 tsp oyster sauce

Place the shiitake mushrooms in a bowl of hot water for 20 minutes to soften and rehydrate. Drain, then finely dice and set aside.

Meanwhile, for the dipping sauce, combine the soy sauce, sugar, oyster sauce and 50ml of water in a small saucepan over low heat. Stir until the sugar has completely dissolved, then remove from the heat and allow to cool. Set aside.

Combine the pork, cornflour and salt in a large bowl and mix well until it has an almost sticky consistency. Squeeze any excess liquid from the shiitake mushroom, then add to the pork mixture along with the prawn, and mix until completely combined. Add the sugar, soy sauce, oyster sauce and oil and mix again until combined. Place the mixture in the fridge for 20 minutes to firm up.

To make the siu mai, set up a dumpling station with the wonton wrappers, pork and prawn mixture and a small bowl of water.

Hold a wonton wrapper in the palm of your hand and place about 1 tbsp of filling in the center. Moisten the edge of the wrapper with water, then cup your hand around the wrapper to bring it together, creating folds in the wrapper skin to form a cup-like shape around the filling. Keep the top of the dumpling exposed.

Place the dumpling on a work surface and press very lightly to flatten the top of the filling (hold the sides while you do this to maintain the cup shape). Place a piece of capsicum on top of the filling, then set aside on a tray. Repeat to make about 35 siu mai.

Bring a large saucepan of water to the boil and line a large bamboo steamer with lettuce leaves or a sheet of baking paper with a few holes cut out.

→

Pork and prawn siu mai continued

Working in batches, arrange the dumplings in the bamboo steamer with 1cm space between each dumpling. Once the water is boiling, place the steamer on top and cover with a lid. Steam the siu mai for 7–8 minutes, until the dumplings are slightly plump.

Add some Lao Gan Ma to the dipping sauce and serve the dumplings straight from the bamboo steamer.

If you'd like to serve the siu mai on a plate, use wet tongs to transfer the dumplings from the bamboo steamer, to stop them sticking.

We like to make a little extra filling and steam it over tofu. This is a really delicious dish that eliminates any waste from the dumpling process. Silken tofu is best. Slice it into 3cm cubes and lay them flat in a ceramic bowl. Bring a small amount of water to the boil in a pot and place the bowl in. Spread your left-over filling on top of the tofu, put the pot lid on and steam for 8–10 minutes. You can add soy for extra flavour. Alternatively, you can stir-fry the filling and serve it in lettuce cups for san choi bao – zero waste!

SPANAKOPITA AND TYROPITA
ANGIE GIANNAKODAKIS, EPOCHA

Prep time 45 minutes

Cook time spanakopita: 35 minutes; tyropita: 20 minutes

Makes 6 spanakopita and 24 tyropita

Spanakopita recipes vary throughout Greece. This version comes from my mama, Katerina, and she makes it for me every week. I always have such a backlog of spanakopita that I can't eat it all. As a good Greek girl, I don't mention it. I just take the food and say, "Thanks Mum."

Mum was born in Athens in 1933 and lived through the Great Depression, World War II and a civil war. She came to Australia just before the rise of the junta. But I think it was more to get away from her parents than a military coup.

I remember my uncle talking about Yiayia's tyropita, which doesn't have spinach and is fried. My mama would make them, but always say, "This was your grandmother's recipe." I didn't realise the importance of that at the time, but for some reason we hide our stories in our food. If you can taste that you'll know where we're from. These are recipes from the heart.

600g plain flour plus extra for dusting

250g (1 cup) Greek yoghurt

120ml extra-virgin olive oil

Poached eggs to serve (optional)

SPANAKOPITA FILLING

1 tbsp extra-virgin olive oil plus extra

1 brown onion roughly chopped

600g English spinach washed and trimmed, roughly chopped

250g Greek feta crumbled

1 tbsp brine from the feta tub

50g dill fronds roughly chopped

Sea salt

TYROPITA FILLING

2 eggs lightly beaten

250g Greek feta crumbled

Greek oregano from a dried bunch, to taste

Sea salt and freshly ground black pepper

Extra-virgin olive oil for shallow-frying

Place the flour, yoghurt and oil in a large bowl. Slowly add 280–300ml of water and bring the ingredients together to form a rough dough (you may not need all the water). Knead the dough in the bowl for 5–7 minutes, until firm and slightly sticky (as ingredients vary throughout the year, be aware that your flour and yoghurt will differ from time to time, so be guided by your instincts). Knead in a little extra flour if necessary, then form into a ball, cover with a clean tea towel or plastic wrap and set aside for 30 minutes.

Preheat the oven to 200°C (fan-forced). Lightly grease a baking tray with oil.

Spanakopita

Pour the oil into a large saucepan and set over medium heat. Add the onion and saute for 5 minutes, until soft and translucent. Add the spinach and saute for 25–30 seconds, until just starting to wilt. Transfer the mixture to a heatproof bowl and allow to cool, then add the feta, brine and dill. Stir gently and season with salt, to taste.

> When buying feta, look for Dodoni or Nikos. You want the feta to be acidic and salty.

Lightly flour a work surface and cut the dough in half. Wrap one half in plastic wrap and set aside in the fridge for the tyropita, another pastry similar to spanakopita. →

Spanakopita and tyropita continued

Roll the remaining dough into three even-sized portions. Working with one portion at a time, roll out the dough to a 30–35cm circle and cut in half. Repeat with the remaining dough.

Liberally scatter the spinach filling over the dough semicircles, leaving a 1cm border along the straight edge, and drizzle with a little olive oil. Starting at the rounded edge, roll up each portion of dough into a cylinder. Trim any excess dough at the ends, then coil the cylinders into six snake-like shapes, tucking the ends under the coils. Transfer to the prepared tray and drizzle with a little oil, then bake for 15 minutes. Reduce the temperature to 180°C (fan-forced) and continue to cook for 20 minutes, or until golden and cooked through.

Allow the spanakopita to cool a little, then serve with a poached egg, if you like.

Tyropita

Cut the remaining dough in half and roll out each half on a lightly floured work surface into a 30cm square.

Combine the egg and feta in a bowl, then rub in a good amount of Greek oregano, a touch of salt and lots of pepper. Stir well to combine, then spread the mixture over one of the dough squares, leaving a 5mm border. Place the remaining dough square on top and press the edges together to seal the filling. Using a sharp knife, divide the dough into 24 diamonds or squares, ensuring that the knife almost seals the edges of each diamond or square as you cut.

> Greek oregano comes on the stalk from Greek delis. Just rub it – it's so much more vibrant than a dry packet from the supermarket.

Heat a large frying pan over medium heat and add enough olive oil to cover the base of the pan. Working in batches, cook the tyropitas for 2–3 minutes each side, until golden and cooked through.

Enjoy with Greek coffee.

MISE PUT

EN IN

PLACE PLACE

By Scott Pickett, Estelle

Mise en place is a French phrase that means "everything in its place", or literally translates to "put in place". It's all the work and preparation that restaurant chefs put in during the day, prior to the arrival of guests and the start of service. If they don't, they're in big trouble.

Mise en place happens first and makes cooking à la minute (to order) much easier, so you're just finishing things off, rather than starting them from scratch. It's making stocks, dicing veggies, assembling garnishes, cleaning and scaling fish. Sometimes things will be portioned and sometimes they'll be left whole, but either way they're ready. Chefs will set up their salt containers, their spoon containers, their utensils, their pots, their pans, their section. They get ready to execute their service.

Mise en place comes from restaurant kitchens, but you should be using it at home, too. It will make you a better cook. When I'm cooking at home, I don't just start my lamb shoulder (page 247) and then get my garlic and whatever. I get everything out and prepare it one by one. In restaurants, we put every prepared element or ingredient in little stainless-steel bowls or plastic containers, but at home I use nice little crockery bowls. I slice my onion, slice my garlic and dice my carrots. I'll do all that, and only then do I start cooking. If you don't already have a set of little bowls, it's worth buying some.

The system is as much a state of mind as it is the physical act of setting up a station in a kitchen. It's also your plan for how you're going to work though the recipe so you don't get halfway through and realise you haven't got the thyme or you haven't got the rosemary or the marjoram. When you're reading the recipe, it helps to visualise each step, including which utensils you'll need for it. Lay them out neatly before you start cooking anything.

Mise en place is also about keeping clean. I'm unbelievably particular about cleaning as I go. In the restaurant, we have little blue cloths folded in a certain way, sitting in a certain spot in the kitchen so that when we cut something, we can wipe our board, wash our hands and then wipe down the bench. The cloth goes back to the same exact spot, so everything stays clean and organised the whole time. When we use a bowl or a pan, we wash them as we go. It's very important and it makes it so much easier working in a clean, controlled space.

Getting into this state of mind will help you execute any recipe quickly, without missing any steps or using any more pots and pans than you need to. And it makes the whole cooking process feel more relaxed and enjoyable, so you'll want to cook more. This in itself makes mise en place invaluable.

VEGET

ABLES

"I use Wijaya curry powder and chilli flakes, a Sri Lankan brand. It's available at Sri Lankan grocery stores, such as Spice Lanka, my brother's store in Glenroy."

RED LENTIL CURRY
SHIYAMALEE SOMAWEERA, CITRUS

Prep time 5 minutes
Cook time 25–30 minutes
Serves 6–8

All the recipes at Citrus, including this one, come from my mother. But I don't cook from written instructions – just memory and taste. I'm always trying to get the same taste I remember from my childhood.

I don't use a lot of oil or salt in this dish. I try to get most of the flavour from the coconut milk. This is "my taste". Our family is from Kandy, in central Sri Lanka. That's why our restaurant logo is an elephant and a Kandyan dancing woman. The food where we're from is not too spicy.

At home, I serve this with mallung (sauteed greens); a fish, chicken or beef curry; coconut sambol; and a few other condiments. And rice, of course.

120ml vegetable oil

1 tsp black mustard seeds

1 tsp cumin seeds

10 fresh curry leaves

1 pandan leaf frozen is fine if you can't find fresh

½ cinnamon quill

3 cloves garlic finely chopped

1 brown onion finely diced

1 tbsp ground turmeric

2 tbsp chilli flakes

1 tbsp curry powder preferably Sri Lankan

2 tsp sweet paprika

500g red lentils rinsed and drained

400ml can coconut milk

Sea salt to taste

Heat the oil in a large saucepan over medium heat. Once the oil is shimmering, add the mustard seeds and cook for 1 minute. Add the cumin seeds, curry leaves, pandan leaf and cinnamon quill and cook for 1 minute until aromatic, then add the garlic, onion and turmeric and cook, stirring occasionally, for 2–3 minutes, until the onion is soft and translucent.

Add the chilli flakes, curry powder, paprika, lentils and 1.5L of water, then reduce the heat to a simmer and cook, stirring occasionally, for 10 minutes or until most of the water has evaporated.

> I taste a dab of the dry spices from the palm of my hand before they go in the pan. I don't use a spoon, as it alters the flavour.

Add the coconut milk, then simmer for a further 8–12 minutes, until the lentils are tender and the curry has a creamy texture. Add salt to taste, then remove from the heat and serve immediately.

LINGUINE WITH FROMAGE FRAIS AND FENNEL
EILEEN HORSNELL, NAPIER QUARTER

Prep time 30 minutes
Cook time 10–15 minutes
Serves 4

When I have people over I usually make pork or fresh pasta. Pasta's really simple, rewarding and impressive. I make the dough in advance and leave it in a lump on the bench. When everyone arrives we roll out the pasta together, which is nice way to involve guests in the meal, and you can be eating within 30 minutes.

This linguine came together around one star ingredient: Holy Goat fromage frais, a low-fat goat's curd that's similar to cottage cheese but without the lumps. It's really beautiful and light, with a citrusy tone, and the runny texture helps the cheese coat the pasta like a sauce. Goat's milk is at its best in spring, so that's the best time to make this dish.

½ bunch **cavolo nero** leaves stripped, finely sliced

2 tbsp **fennel seeds** lightly toasted

2 tsp **chilli flakes** lightly toasted

2 tbsp **salted butter**

1 **fennel bulb** finely sliced

4 cloves **garlic** finely sliced

4 **golden shallots** finely sliced

150ml **white wine**

400g **fresh linguine**

100g **Grana Padano** finely grated

100g **pitted black olives** chopped (or 10 anchovy fillets)

Zest and juice of 1 **lemon**

Sea salt and freshly ground black pepper

50ml **extra-virgin olive oil**

150g **fromage frais**

¼ bunch **parsley** leaves picked and chopped

Blanch the cavolo nero in a large saucepan of salted boiling water for 2 minutes, then drain, refresh under cold running water and set aside.

Refill the pan with water, set over high heat and bring to the boil, adding a good pinch of salt.

Meanwhile, finely grind the toasted fennel seeds using a mortar and pestle and combine with the chilli flakes.

Heat a large frying pan over medium heat, add the butter and melt for 3–4 minutes until foaming. Add the fennel and saute for 7–8 minutes, until transparent, then add the garlic and shallot and saute for 5–7 minutes, until lightly caramelised. Add the wine and cook until reduced by two thirds.

Next, place the pasta in the boiling water – this will only take around 2 minutes to cook, so from now we have to work quickly.

Add the Grana Padano to the fennel mixture so it gets a little melty, then grab a small ladle and pour in about 50ml of cooking water from the pasta pan. Quickly drain the pasta and add to the pan, along with the cavolo nero, then stir through the spices, olives and lemon zest and juice, and season with salt and pepper.

> If using anchovies instead of olives, I recommend Olasagasti as they're extremely meaty. If you can't find these, any good-quality Spanish anchovy fillets will work.

Divide the pasta among four plates and drizzle over the olive oil. Garnish with the fromage frais and parsley and serve.

"You can find Holy Goat cheeses at farmers' markets in and around Melbourne. Check the Holy Goat website to see which farmers' market they're at each week."

CHONGQING NOODLES
SHANNON MARTINEZ, SMITH & DAUGHTERS

Prep time 20 minutes

Cook time 15 minutes

Serves 4

Sichuan food is like a drug. I get withdrawals when I don't have it. I think it has something to do with the numbing Sichuan pepper. Normally, I eat it once a week, and my favourite restaurants are Sichuan House and Tina's Noodle Kitchen.

During Melbourne's lockdown, I was going through chemo. My immunity was compromised and I wasn't allowed to leave the house. Neither restaurant could deliver to me, so I had to come up with this recipe.

The chemo really affected my tastebuds and I needed things that were extra punchy and extra spicy. This dish is that at the best of times. It's definitely not for the faint of heart, that's for sure.

3 tbsp copha or vegetable oil

250g vegan mince

2.5cm piece of ginger peeled and grated

2 cloves garlic finely chopped

40g (¼ cup) chopped zha cai

1 tsp chilli flakes

2 spring onions white and green parts finely sliced and kept separate

2 tbsp Shaoxing rice wine

2 tbsp tian mian jiang

400g cooked wide wheat noodles

2 bok choy quartered and blanched

Chopped roasted peanuts to serve

Coriander leaves to serve

CHONGQING NOODLE BROTH

800ml vegan chicken or vegetable stock

400g can chickpeas or cooked white peas (see note)

2.5cm piece of ginger peeled and julienned

2 cloves garlic finely chopped

3 tbsp light soy sauce

3 tbsp Sichuan chilli oil

1 tbsp Chinkiang black vinegar

1 tbsp doubanjiang

1 tbsp sesame oil

1 tsp red Sichuan peppercorns toasted and ground

½ tsp sugar optional

Heat a wok or large heavy-based frying pan over high heat, then add the copha or vegetable oil. Add the mince and cook, breaking up any larger pieces with the back of a wooden spoon, for 4–5 minutes, until starting to brown.

> You can get V2 mince from most major supermarkets. It's made in Australia. Vegan food isn't just about animal welfare, but also environmental issues, so it's important to buy local.

Stir through the ginger, garlic, zha cai, chilli flakes and white part of the spring onion and saute for 30 seconds, then add the Shaoxing rice wine and tian mian jiang. Continue to saute for 3–4 minutes, until the mixture becomes dry. Transfer to a bowl and set aside.

> Asian grocers sell little pouches of zha cai, or Sichuan pickle, for about 70 cents. While you're there pick up the tian mian jiang (sweet bean paste) and doubanjiang (fermented chilli bean paste).

Meanwhile, to make the noodle broth, place the stock and chickpeas in a saucepan and bring to the boil over high heat. Reduce the heat to a low simmer and cook, uncovered, for 5 minutes. Add the remaining broth ingredients and stir through to combine.

> White peas are traditional but tricky to find. If you can find them, use them instead of chickpeas. Usually they come dried and you cook them like any dried pulse.

To serve, divide the noodles among four large bowls, then pour over the broth. Top with the mince mixture, blanched bok choy, green spring onion, chopped roasted peanuts and coriander leaves.

> If you like it extra spicy, serve with prickly ash oil (often sold as Sichuan peppercorn oil). It's optional but fun.

ESSENTIAL

KITCHEN

TOOLS

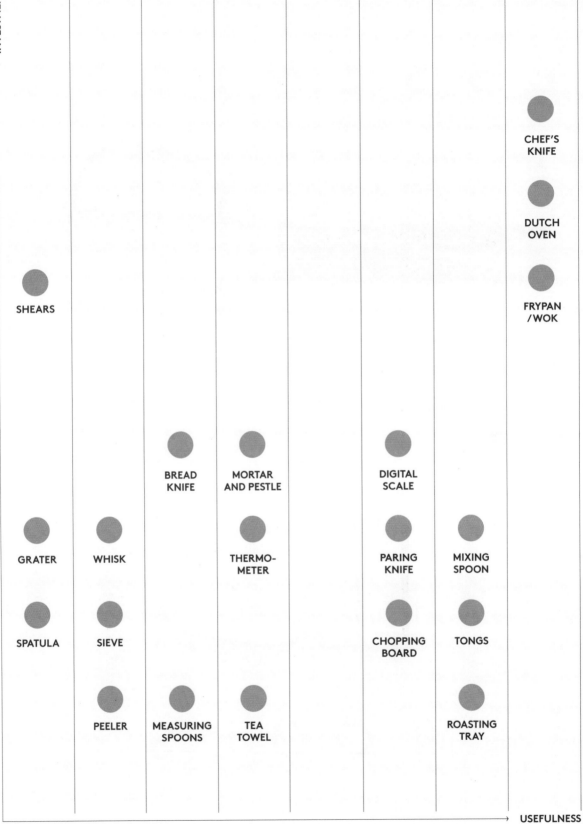

INVESTMENT

USEFULNESS

CHEF'S
KNIFE

DUTCH
OVEN

FRYPAN
/WOK

SHEARS

BREAD
KNIFE

MORTAR
AND PESTLE

DIGITAL
SCALE

GRATER

WHISK

THERMO-
METER

PARING
KNIFE

MIXING
SPOON

SPATULA

SIEVE

CHOPPING
BOARD

TONGS

PEELER

MEASURING
SPOONS

TEA
TOWEL

ROASTING
TRAY

Buy your gear at a proper restaurant supply store such as Cedar Hospitality in Brunswick, Hotel Agencies in Fitzroy or Chef's Hat in South Melbourne. These sorts of places are more affordable and stock nothing but durable, functional equipment that goes the distance.

BREAD KNIFE This long serrated knife is more useful than most home cooks might guess. In addition to slicing bread, it can be used to cut fruit and vegetables with tough or slippery skins, such as pumpkin, watermelon and pineapple. And cakes, too, of course.

CHEF'S KNIFE Used for the vast majority of chopping tasks, a chef's knife is the main thing worth investing in. Shop in person for reputable European and Japanese brands such as Wüsthof, Zwilling/JA Henckels, Sabatier, Misono, Shun and Global, and find something that feels comfortable and balanced in your hand. Hone your knife on a steel regularly (this won't wear it out or damage it), get it sharpened professionally about once a year, never put it in the dishwasher, and it'll basically last forever.

DUTCH OVEN Le Creuset, Staub and Chasseur are three of the leading brands when it comes to this workhorse pot. Made of hefty cast iron and enamelled for a slick, easy-to-clean surface, this lifetime piece is solid enough to slow-cook and properly brown meat; large enough for soups, stocks and stews; and rugged enough for deep-frying or placing directly in the oven.

FOOD THERMOMETER Don't wonder if your steak is cooked rare or medium-rare. Know. A cheap digital probe thermometer lets you measure the internal temperature – and thus, the "doneness" – instantly. Likewise, if you plan on making any kind of confectionary, a candy thermometer is a must.

FRYING PAN Carbon steel and cast iron have their advantages, but they're heavy and need special care. For everyday use, a roughly 25cm stainless steel or anodised aluminium skillet is tough, easy to clean and will last for a decade or more.

GRATER You will need two different types: a durable box grater for slicing and coarsely grating fruit, vegetables and cheese, and the finer rasp grater (often called "Microplane", after the most famous brand), which is ideal for zesting citrus, grating nutmeg, mincing garlic and other such fiddly tasks.

MORTAR AND PESTLE They may have a point or they may just be purists, but either way, some very notable chefs, such as Thai authority David Thompson, swear that no spice grinder, blender or food processor can achieve the same results as a good mortar and pestle. Look for one made of solid granite and you can't go too wrong.

PARING KNIFE At roughly half the size of the chef's knife, the paring knife is made for delicate work such as deseeding vegetables and deveining prawns. You don't need to spend big here, but treat it with the same care as your chef's knife.

PEELER Yes, it peels carrots and potatoes. But you can also use it to neatly shave chocolate, fridge-cold butter and hard cheeses such as parmesan. Chefs tend to favour Y-shaped peelers over straight peelers, due to their larger grips and general versatility. A cheapie will do.

SHEARS Knives can do almost everything. But when it comes to cutting through a chicken's breastbone, snipping herbs, opening packaging or chopping canned fruit without taking it out of the can, you need a sturdy set of kitchen scissors. As with your chef's knife, look for European and Japanese brands such as Wüsthof and Shun, which will hold their edge longer and may even come apart to facilitate sharpening.

TEA TOWEL A tea towel is a tea towel is a tea towel, right? Yes. But like the bread knife, it has more uses than it's usually given credit for – drying dishes being the least handy. Laid flat, it can stabilise chopping boards (warped ones especially) and prevent them from slipping around on your bench. Knotted on a pot handle, it creates a safe, heat-free grip. And it can be used to pat down moist meat or veggies, saving paper towels from landfill. Keep a dozen or so 100 per cent cotton towels in rotation.

WOK Wok hei, or "breath of the wok" is the distinctive smoky character that rolls off a fresh stir-fry and makes it taste so special. At home it's almost impossible to heat your wok hot enough to start the right chemical reactions. Regardless, a good wok should retain as much heat as possible, which counts out aluminium and stainless steel. A carbon steel wok with a wooden handle is the way to go, and you might want to think about a lid. Regularly season the surface with oil and it'll last forever.

MINESTRONE
RITA MACALI, SUPERMAXI

Prep time 12–15 minutes
Cook time 1 hour 10 minutes
Serves 6

There are two things that inspire me to make this minestrone: cold, rainy weather, and a particular plate of my grandmother's which is now in my possession. If I see this plate on a winter's day, it's guaranteed that I instantly want to make this soup!

I use short pasta in this recipe, such as ditali, or my personal favourite, "mista", which consists of broken-up and left-over bits of pasta from different packets. You can usually find it in the pasta section at delicatessens, or you can make your own by simply breaking up any left-over bits and bobs of pasta sitting at the back of the pantry.

There's no need to use vegetable stock here, as the soup makes its own delicious broth as it cooks.

3 tbsp extra-virgin olive oil
2 cloves garlic peeled and smashed
1 brown onion diced (optional)
150g potato cut into bite-sized chunks
200g (1 cup) canned crushed tomatoes
200g (1 cup) canned lentils drained
180g (1 cup) canned chickpeas drained
170g (1 cup) canned cannellini beans drained
125g zucchini cut into bite-sized chunks
85g (1 cup) chopped savoy cabbage
65g cauliflower florets cut into bite-sized chunks
Handful of fresh basil leaves
Sea salt and freshly ground black pepper
50–55g ditali pasta

TO SERVE
Grated parmesan
Extra-virgin olive oil
Finely diced long red chilli optional

Heat the oil and garlic in a large heavy-based saucepan over medium heat and cook for 5 minutes or until the garlic is golden brown. Remove using a slotted spoon and discard.

Add the onion, if using, and saute for 6–7 minutes, until soft. Add the potato and crushed tomatoes and stir for about 1 minute, then add the tinned legumes, remaining vegetables and basil.

> The secret to this soup is to boil it rapidly from the start so the beans and potato break down, leaving you with a wonderfully thick, creamy soup.

Cover with 1.5–1.8L of water, season generously with salt and pepper and bring to the boil. Cook, stirring frequently so the ingredients don't stick and burn on the base of the pan, for about 1 hour, until the vegetables are completely soft.

Towards the end of the cooking time, add the pasta and cook according to the packet instructions (don't overcook). Taste and season with more salt and pepper if needed.

Ladle the soup into bowls and top with some grated parmesan, a drizzle of extra-virgin olive oil and maybe some chopped fresh chilli.

CHICKPEA BAKE
HANA ASSAFIRI, MOROCCAN SOUP BAR

Prep time 15 minutes, plus overnight soaking

Cook time 45 minutes

Serves 4–6

I have always called this dish "chickpea bake", although it's similar to fatteh, which is made in cuisines spanning the Arab and Middle Eastern worlds. Some people make fatteh with lamb and beef instead of chickpeas, some people make it with just chickpeas, some people don't use any nuts, some people do. Fatteh just means bread soaked in juices and I do the contrary – I don't soak the bread at all. I keep the flatbread crisp.

I make this dish in a particular way because I'm vegetarian and have been for more than 40 years. In all our dishes, we experiment and tweak to create depths of flavour and to make sure nutrition is satisfied.

For me, this dish is the people's hero; they have decided that the chickpea bake is the standout dish over and above everything else we serve at Moroccan Soup Bar. People love it. It's been described as anything from an "orchestra in your mouth", to tacos, lasagne and chickpea salad. I think it's the crazy combination of flavours – it tastes a bit like a dessert because of the caramelised nuts in butter, which just make it sing. I'm never reticent to share the recipe because it belongs to the community that gave it the status.

1½ cups dried chickpeas or 3 cups cooked chickpeas

2 large round flatbreads

200g salted butter melted

2–3 tsp salt flakes

5 cloves garlic

300g plain yoghurt

1 tbsp tahini

100g slivered almonds

1 tsp sweet smoked paprika

2 tbsp finely chopped parsley to serve

If using dried chickpeas, place them in a large bowl, cover with cold water and leave overnight to plump up. The next day, drain and rinse the chickpeas, discarding the soaking water.

Place the chickpeas in a large saucepan and cover with plenty of cold water (you can skip this step if using pre-cooked chickpeas). Bring to the boil over high heat and cook for 30–40 minutes, until softened. (The time will vary depending on the size of the chickpeas, so check them every 15 minutes to ensure they remain covered with water and don't overcook.) Drain and set aside.

Meanwhile, preheat the oven to 250°C.

Place the flatbreads directly on an oven shelf and toast for 8–10 minutes. Remove from the oven, place on a large baking tray and generously brush with some of the melted butter. Sprinkle with a pinch of salt flakes, then return to the oven and toast for a further 4–5 minutes.

Remove the tray from the oven, turn the flatbreads over and generously brush with a little more melted butter. Sprinkle with another pinch of salt flakes and return to the oven for another 4–5 minutes.

When the bread has finished toasting, break it into corn chip–sized pieces, and place in a shallow serving dish. Set aside.

→

Vegetables

"I cook to smell and taste, so my cooking methods differ to the metric measure of ingredients. This recipe is an overview and you should change it to suit your taste. For example, you can add more yoghurt if need be. And when all else fails, add more butter."

Chickpea bake continued

Place the garlic and remaining salt in a mortar and use the pestle to crush the garlic to a smooth paste. Transfer to a small bowl, add the yoghurt and tahini and stir to combine.

Place the remaining butter in a small frying pan over medium heat. Add the slivered almonds and cook for 1.5–2 minutes, until golden brown, fragrantly nutty and almost caramelised. Immediately remove from the heat.

Working quickly, spoon the hot, just-cooked chickpeas over the toasted buttery flatbread, then thickly cover with the garlicky yoghurt mixture and sprinkle the paprika on top.

While still nice and hot, pour the melted butter and almonds over the yoghurt topping – it should make a "tsh" sound when the hot butter meets the cold yoghurt. Sprinkle with the chopped parsley, and enjoy.

> This dish can easily be made vegan by using tahini in place of yoghurt. But you have to create the same texture as yoghurt by adding garlic, lemon and salt, thinning it down with chickpea brine and whizzing it together. Replace the butter with vegan butter or oil.

Vegetables

"Don't be afraid of taking shortcuts. Don't be a hero. Even professional chefs use canned beans. Don't think everything has to be from scratch; it doesn't make you better. Just chill out."

KASHMIRI PANEER
DOUGAL COLAM, BHANG

Prep time 15 minutes
Cook time 25 minutes
Serves 4

In my early twenties, a long time ago now, I was lucky enough to visit Kashmir with some friends. I love the mountains. It's beautiful up there and very different from down south. One of the guys was a photographer for a ski magazine. There were no tracks on the slopes in Kashmir so you could get some awesome photos. I was just tagging along because it seemed really exciting.

We hired a houseboat on Dal Lake, because that was the only accommodation available. They all had little heaters in them and stuff like that, so they were pretty comfy. And the boat came with a cook.

I've never forgotten the fragrant and delicious meals we enjoyed on that boat. This Kashmiri paneer recipe is from that region, and now we serve it at Bhang. It's a pretty simple recipe, the only thing that's really important to get right is that you have to cook the mustard oil until it's smoking. It cooks a lot of the bitterness out and improves the flavour.

80ml (⅓ cup) mustard oil
400g paneer cut into 1cm cubes
Pinch of ground asafoetida
4 cloves
2 cinnamon quills
6 green cardamom pods
3 dried bay leaves
½ tsp caraway seeds
400g can pureed tomatoes
2 tsp ground ginger
1 tsp fennel seeds ground using a mortar and pestle
½ tsp Kashmiri chilli powder
3 tbsp plain yoghurt whisked
6 saffron threads
1 tbsp roughly chopped coriander leaves
Sea salt to taste
1 tbsp pouring or thickened cream
Steamed basmati rice or naan bread to serve

Heat 2 tbsp of the mustard oil in a heavy-based frying pan over medium heat until slightly smoking. Add the paneer and saute for 5–6 minutes, until golden, then transfer to a bowl of warm water, along with the asafoetida, and set aside (this will soften the paneer).

Heat the remaining 2 tbsp of mustard oil until slightly smoking again, then remove from the heat and let it cool a little. Add the whole spices, return the pan to medium heat and saute for 1–2 minutes, until the cardamom pods start popping and releasing their aroma.

Add the pureed tomatoes, ground ginger, ground fennel and chilli powder and stir to combine, then add the yoghurt and saffron threads. Mix well, then simmer for 5–10 minutes, until slightly thickened, fragrant and the oil has started to separate from the mixture. Drain the paneer and stir into the tomato mixture. Simmer for a minute or two to warm through.

Add the coriander leaves and salt to taste, then transfer to a serving dish and drizzle the cream over the top. Enjoy with steamed basmati rice or warm bread.

Vegetables

TWO EASY
DINNERS YOUR
KIDS WILL LOVE
TO EAT

KIDS
IN THE KITCHEN
(AND HELP MAKE)

ROAST CHICKEN WRAPS
BENJAMIN COOPER, CHIN CHIN

Prep time 15 minutes | **Serves** 5

This dinner is less of a recipe and more of a way to evolve your kids' idea of food. Sometimes the best way to get your kids to be more adventurous with what they eat is by not forcing them to try things, but by having those ingredients present as part of your daily eating habits.

My wife and I have found that this is one of those sorts of dining experiences where everyone can eat the same core meal and then through condiments, seasonings and relishes, you can all be adventurous and create your own fun. It's quick, it's easy and most of all it's delicious.

---

1 store-bought whole roast chicken

1–2 **Lebanese cucumbers** sliced

200g **hummus** we devour this, so if your family is the same, you may need a lot more

200g baby spinach leaves

5–10 **slices of cheese** we use cheddar or Jarlsberg depending on the night

100g **your favourite tomato relish or salsa**

5–10 large or 15–20 small flatbreads, soft flour tortillas or rotis

TOASTED SESAME SALT

2 tbsp white sesame seeds

1 tbsp sea salt flakes

OPTIONAL EXTRAS

Chilli flakes, sriracha, Kewpie mayonnaise, wasabi paste, roast eggplant, furikake, pickled chillies, avocado, ajvar, tzatziki, hot chips or baked sweet potato chips, tahini, pickles, and herbs from your own garden

---

Grab a roast chicken from your favourite local (with minimum chips). Get the kids to shred the chicken and set it aside, while you're organising the rest of the ingredients. My youngest loves to help slice ingredients on his own chopping board using a butter knife. (As he got older I taught him how to use one of my vegetable knives, always under supervision.)

To make the toasted sesame salt, put both ingredients in a pan over a low heat and toss until the seeds are golden and fragrant. Pound using a mortar and pestle until the mix is 50/50 coarse and fine. This is delicious on almost anything.

Lay out all your small bowls and fill each one with a specific ingredient. Then add in any of the extras that you feel like (go crazy and add them all if you feel like it). Place all of the ingredients in the middle of the table – it will look like an epic smorgasbord. Let everyone to build their own wrap.

CHICKEN AND VEGETABLE DUMPLINGS
SHANE DELIA, MAHA

Prep time 35 minutes | **Cook time** 24 minutes | **Makes** 50 dumplings

Dumplings are great for kids. I like to make them with whatever veggies I've got in the fridge. Zucchini, kale, squash, cabbage, carrot, celery and spring onion all work great. Because the dumplings are all wrapped up, the kids don't know what's inside.

You can make the filling with your kids, or pre-make it so they don't see what's in there. My daughter, she'd eat it all. My son, it's usually best just to hide it from him. When he says, "What's all that stuff?" you can just say, "That's all the stuff that goes in cheeseburgers." Or whatever you need to sell the dream.

I try to make my dumplings quite bland on the inside. Even though they're my kids and they should know how to eat better, they do quite like bland flavours.

¼ white, savoy or Chinese cabbage chopped

1 carrot peeled and roughly chopped

¼ stick celery roughly chopped

3 spring onions roughly chopped

2cm piece of ginger peeled and roughly chopped

Handful of shiitake or enoki mushrooms

1 skinless chicken breast

2 egg whites

1 tsp salt

1 tsp caster sugar optional

½ tsp sesame oil

2 tbsp cornflour

50 store-bought dumpling wrappers

DRESSING

100ml soy sauce

3 tbsp Chinese vinegar

1 tsp sesame oil

1 tbsp sugar

1 tbsp chilli oil for the adults, optional for kids

1 bunch coriander finely chopped (for the adults, optional for kids)

Place the veggies, ginger and mushrooms in a food processor and pulse for a few seconds. Don't puree the vegetables. You want them to still have a bit of size and texture, but be fine enough to hide from the kids. Transfer the veggies to a large mixing bowl.

Place the chicken breast, egg whites, salt, sugar (if using) and sesame oil in a food processor. Whizz until it forms a thick paste. This is your binding agent for the veggies. Add the chicken mixture to the bowl with the veggies and mix thoroughly using a spoon or spatula. Kids love to help with this step.

Put a large pot of water on to boil, or set up a steamer basket over a pot of boiling water. Mix the cornflour and 2 tbsp of water together in a small bowl to make a slurry. This will help the dumplings seal up nice and tight. Place 1–2 tbsp of the filling in each dumpling wrapper. Dip your fingers into the slurry, fold each dumpling into a half-moon shape and pinch the edges closed firmly. Little hands are good for this.

Boil or steam the dumplings in batches for 6–8 minutes at a time, or until the insides are cooked. Try not to crowd the pot or steamer too much. Uncooked dumplings will freeze well for use down the track. Make the dipping sauce by whisking together all the ingredients in a small bowl. Pour over the cooked dumplings, or put on the table for everyone to dip as they like.

SEAFO

OD

Seafood

WHOLE BAKED FLOUNDER
MICHAEL BACASH, BACASH

Prep time 5 minutes
Cook time 15 minutes
Serves 2

A lot of what I know about fish and what we do at Bacash, I just can't put into words. Some of the best stuff we do has nothing to do with recipes, but more to do with an innate understanding of fish: the different species and how they react to heat and different cooking techniques.

This understanding of fish isn't a gift. It's not something I've studied. It's just accumulated from my childhood spent fishing off Mount Martha Beach, where we still have a boatshed. I grew up knowing fresh fish in a way you can only understand when you've caught it. A chef who has never caught a fish will always be at least two or three days behind the game.

The way to tell if a fish is fresh is best explained this way: imagine walking into a pet shop, taking a fish out of the tank and putting it on the bench. Its colour is vibrant and there's life in its eyes. You put it back in the water, and it swims away. Now think of a fish at the market. How close to that just-out-of-the-water look is the fish in the display? You're looking for firm, bright eyes and the fish should be slim, firm and robust, not limp and dull.

At Bacash we think the best flounder is New Zealand yellowbelly flounder. Our method of grilling is really about minimal interference.

Butter for greasing and cooking
1 x 450–500g yellowbelly flounder
Sea salt
Handful of flat-leaf parsley leaves chopped
½ lemon
Fries to serve

Preheat the oven to 200°C. Grease a baking tray with butter.

Heat a heavy-based frying pan over high heat (you don't want the fish to cool down the pan when it makes contact, so make sure it's really hot).

Make several shallow incisions on each side of the fish where the flesh is thickest.

> There's no need to scale the fish. The scales are unnoticeable when cooked and removing them only risks damaging the flesh unnecessarily.

Season the fish with salt. When seasoning a stew or similar, it doesn't really matter where you season, but a piece of fish is different. Imagine a grid on the surface of the fish, and season every square evenly.

Place the fish in the pan and sear for 1 minute on each side. Pay close attention to the fins and remove the fish from the pan once they begin to brown.

Transfer the fish to the prepared tray, add 1 tsp of butter to the scored surface and place the tray in the oven. The aim here is to heat the centre of the fish without cooking it further.

→

Footscray Market, Footscray

Whole baked flounder continued

If it gets to the same temperature as the oven, it will be way overcooked. Every oven is different and you'd think that 200°C is 200°C, but that's not necessarily the case.

Heat the fish for 4–5 minutes, but check it frequently throughout this time and take it out when the centre is still a little translucent.

> Don't trust your timer. It can tell you how long the fish has been in the oven, but it will never tell you if the fish is cooked. I've spent 20 years trying to tell new people in my kitchen to stop using timers, but it's so ingrained into young chefs that it's an impossible task. Apparently I'm a dinosaur.

Sprinkle liberally with the parsley and serve with the lemon and a side of hot fries.

SPANISH MACKEREL MARINATED IN ANDALUSIAN SPICES
FRANK CAMORRA, MOVIDA

Prep time 15 minutes, plus at least 3 hours marinating

Cook time 1 hour

Serves 6

If I'm at home on the weekend, I like to visit Queen Victoria Market on a Sunday morning to find something tasty to cook. On one occasion, I found some amazing Spanish mackerel "darnes" (fish cutlets). I love this fish. It's beautifully oily and has a strong taste that stands up to big Spanish flavours. I decided to create a mash-up of two traditional Andalusian dishes: cazón en adobo and salsa rotena. Cazón en adobo is a classic southern Spanish dish (the name changes depending on the town), where dogfish is marinated in Moorish spices before frying it; something we've been doing at Movida Lorne since the start with local gummy shark. Salsa rotena is taken from an old-fashioned fisherman's dish in the south, where they traditionally braise sea bass in a thick stew of tomato and sherry.

In this dish, the adobo marinade brings all those aromatic Andalusian, Moorish spices that I love, while the sherry vinegar holds the acidity, balancing the fat of the fish. And with a semolina crumb, the fish keeps intact and cooks perfectly, falling off the bone with ease when you cut into it. The rich tomato and sherry sauce wonderfully contrasts the texture and spices of the fried mackerel cutlets. Served with a green side salad and bread, it's simply delicious.

6 x 250–280g Spanish mackerel cutlets

500g fine semolina

1L extra-virgin olive oil for frying

Mixed salad leaves to serve

Crusty bread to serve

ADOBO

2½ tbsp cumin seeds

2 tbsp sweet smoked paprika

2 tbsp dried oregano

½ brown onion finely sliced

3 cloves garlic finely chopped

200ml sherry vinegar

1 tsp sea salt

1 tsp freshly ground black pepper

1 cup flat-leaf parsley finely chopped

→

Preheat the oven to 170°C.

To make the adobo, place the cumin seeds on a small baking tray, then transfer to the oven and cook for 6 minutes until lightly toasted. Transfer to a spice grinder and grind to a fine powder. Tip the ground cumin into a large bowl, add the remaining adobo ingredients and 700ml of water, stirring to combine. Add the mackerel and stir to coat in the adobo, then cover, transfer to the fridge and marinate for 3–4 hours or overnight.

> Spanish mackerel cutlets are accessible almost all year round. Don't be afraid to ask your fishmonger if you can smell the fish – the longer the fish has been exposed to air or left sitting out, the smellier it becomes.

To make the salsa rotena, pour the olive oil into a large heavy-based saucepan and set over medium–low heat. Add the onion and a pinch of salt and cook, stirring occasionally, for 10 minutes, until soft but not coloured (the salt helps the onion sweat without colouring). Add the garlic and bay leaves and cook for 3 minutes, then add the capsicum and cook for 10 minutes or until soft. Add the sherry, then increase the heat to medium–high and cook for 3 minutes until the liquid is reduced. Add the tomatoes and pepper, reduce the heat to medium–low heat and cook, stirring occasionally, for 30 minutes until well reduced. Set aside and keep warm.

→

SALSA ROTENA

200ml olive oil

1 large brown onion finely diced

Sea salt

3 cloves garlic finely diced

3 fresh bay leaves

1 green capsicum finely diced

250ml fino sherry

2 x 400g cans crushed tomatoes

Pinch of freshly ground black pepper

Spanish mackerel marinated in Andalusian spices continued

Tip the semolina onto a large tray. Heat the oil in a large heavy-based saucepan over medium heat to 180–190°C on a kitchen thermometer.

Remove the mackerel from the marinade, gently shake off any excess and completely coat in the semolina. Working in two or three batches, carefully fry the mackerel for 4–5 minutes, then gently turn over and cook for a further 4–5 minutes, until well browned and cooked through. Remove the mackerel with a slotted spoon and drain on a tray of paper towel to absorb the excess oil. Season with salt.

Place one juicy piece of fried mackerel onto six plates and spoon a ladleful of salsa rotena on top. Serve with a few green leaves and some bread to mop up the sauce.

Ocean Made Seafood, Collingwood

GUAJILLO OCTOPUS TACOS
MATT LANE, MAMASITA

Prep time 15 minutes,
plus overnight freezing

Cook time 1 hour

Serves 4

In my family this is a real staple comfort food. My wife is pescatarian so we eat a lot of seafood at home. Her background is Spanish, and this dish started with us making a standard Galician octopus with paprika and potatoes. Our kids love tacos and live on them, and it just evolved from there. Guajillo is a type of Mexican chilli I like, similar to paprika – it's mild and slightly sweet, but with an earthiness to it.

In summer we usually boil the octopus and then finish it off on the barbie, making the most of the weather and eating outside. However, it's easy to dry out the octopus if you cook it for too long on the grill. I usually fire the barbie super hot – 250 or 300 degrees – then chuck on the octopus and wait for it to char up and get a bit crisp. No longer than that.

In winter, I can't be bothered standing outside in the freezing cold, so we just boil it for about an hour. It's one of those good cold-weather dishes that fills the house with a nice aroma.

4 large octopus tentacles about 1kg

1 orange cut into 6–8 slices

1 red onion cut into 6–8 slices

3–4 dried bay leaves

500g nicola or dutch cream potatoes unpeeled, cut into bite-sized cubes

2 tbsp olive oil

2 mild or spicy chorizo sausages casings removed

Sea salt and freshly ground black pepper

12 large corn tortillas La Tortilleria make the best, but supermarket ones are fine

3 limes quartered

GUAJILLO SALSA

4 dried guajillo chillies

120ml olive oil

1 brown onion diced

2 cloves garlic finely chopped

1 tsp cumin seeds

½ tsp black peppercorns

Buy the octopus tentacles the day before and freeze them overnight – I find octopus is more tender if cooked after being frozen.

Bring a large saucepan of water to the boil over high heat and add the orange, red onion and bay leaves. Add the octopus tentacles, then reduce the heat to a simmer and cook for 45–60 minutes, until tender. Drain and allow to cool slightly, then chop the octopus into bite-sized pieces.

You can also chargrill the octopus to get it nice and crispy. To do this, let the octopus cool for 20–30 minutes out of the pot. Preheat a barbeque grill plate to high. Pour olive oil over the octopus legs, then cut into manageable pieces for tongs. Grill for a few minutes each side or until charred and crisp, then combine in the bowl with the potato and chorizo.

To make the guajillo salsa, remove the stalks and seeds from the chillies, then lightly toast in a frying pan over medium heat for 2–3 minutes, until fragrant and slightly charred.

Heat the olive oil in a saucepan over medium heat and add the onion, garlic, cumin seeds and peppercorns. Saute for 8–10 minutes, until caramelised, then add the toasted chillies and 125ml (½ cup) of water. Bring to the boil, then reduce the heat to a simmer and cook for 20 minutes. Remove from the heat and allow to cool, then blitz in a blender to make a smooth salsa. Transfer to a serving bowl. →

Guajillo octopus tacos continued

If you can't be bothered making the guajillo salsa, simply add a generous amount of smoked paprika and olive oil to the potato and chorizo mixture before adding the octopus. Add chopped parsley or any store-bought salsa verde at the end of cooking. This makes a very tasty Spanish-style substitute.

Meanwhile, cook the potato in a saucepan of salted boiling water for 6–7 minutes until tender. Drain and set aside.

Heat the oil in a large frying pan over medium heat. Crumble in the chorizo and saute for 5 minutes until browned. Add the potato and stir through for 1–2 minutes to coat in the chorizo oil, then add the octopus and stir through for a further 1 minute. Season with salt and pepper to taste. Keep warm.

Heat a dry frying pan over medium heat and, working in batches, cook the tortillas for 30 seconds each side until warm and floppy – don't overcook them or they'll become hard. Remove and place in a tea towel to keep warm.

To serve, place the octopus mixture in a serving dish in the centre of the table, along with the warm tortillas and guajillo salsa. Invite guests to fill their tortillas with the octopus, chorizo and potato mix, a little guajillo salsa and a squeeze of lime.

Leftovers? Make the best quesadillas you'll ever eat. Simply lay a tortilla in a frying pan over low heat and sprinkle a little cheese over the top. Fill half the tortilla with the octopus mix, then fold it in half and cook on both sides until the cheese oozes out. Enjoy!

CLAY-POT FISH WITH PEPPERBERRY AND CRISPY PORK LARD
KHANH NGUYEN, SUNDA

Prep time 20 minutes

Cook time 45 minutes

Serves 2–4

This fish recipe is one of my favourite Vietnamese dishes to cook on my days off. It's quick, easy and so delicious. It's quite a traditional recipe, similar to one my mum used to cook when I lived at home in Sydney. I like to add native Australian pepperberry as it adds a unique aroma, which I think takes this dish to another level.

Traditionally, when families would buy fish whole, this dish would be eaten with a sweet and sour tamarind soup made from the offcuts. I just use cutlets for this recipe, which I fry before adding to the braise – this adds a beautiful crust, which not only gives you great texture but helps the fish absorb all the flavours, too.

400–500g barramundi or salmon cutlets look for 1 large or 2 smaller cutlets

Sea salt and freshly ground black pepper

1L vegetable oil for deep-frying

60g rice flour

160g caster sugar

1 large tomato diced

½ large banana shallot roughly chopped

10 cloves garlic roughly chopped

5cm piece of ginger peeled and finely sliced

1 small long red chilli finely sliced

1½ tbsp light soy sauce

25ml fish sauce

250ml (1 cup) coconut water

2 tsp black peppercorns crushed

½ tsp ground pepperberry

2 spring onions finely sliced

1 tbsp crispy fried shallots

3–4 sprigs coriander cut into 3cm lengths

Steamed rice or salad to serve

CRISPY PORK LARD

200g pork back fat cut into 1–2cm cubes

2 tbsp vegetable oil

Season both sides of the fish cutlets with salt and pepper, then set aside for 15 minutes. This ensures the fish will be seasoned the whole way through rather than just the surface. Be generous with your seasoning – I recommend 1 tsp of salt each side – as it will impart flavour throughout the whole dish when cooked in the caramel.

Meanwhile, heat the vegetable oil in a large saucepan over medium heat to 180°C on a kitchen thermometer.

Lightly dust the fish cutlets with the rice flour, then add to the oil and deep-fry for 2 minutes each side. Remove from the oil using a slotted spoon and drain the fish on paper towels or a wire rack with paper towel underneath. Set aside until ready to use.

To make the crispy pork lard, combine the pork back fat and oil in a small saucepan and cook over medium–low heat for 25–30 minutes, until the fat renders and you have beautifully golden, crispy pieces of lard. Remove the lard from the oil and drain on paper towel, then set aside. Keep the rendered pork fat in the pan and reheat over low heat just before serving.

Combine the sugar and 80ml (⅓ cup) of water in a large clay pot or heavy-based saucepan and set over low heat. Once the sugar has melted, increase the heat to high and bring the sugar syrup to the boil. After 5–7 minutes, the sugar will start to caramelise around the side of the pot or pan. Keep cooking until the syrup turns golden brown or reaches 165°C on a kitchen thermometer. If the sugar starts to caramelise unevenly, gently swirl the pot or pan in a circular motion to distribute the sugar.

→

Clay-pot fish with pepperberry and crispy pork lard continued

Once the sugar is caramelised, add the tomato, shallot, garlic, ginger and chilli. Cook for 1–2 minutes, until softened, then add the soy sauce, fish sauce, coconut water, black peppercorns and pepperberry. Bring to the boil, then add the fish and reduce the heat to a simmer. Cover and cook for 15 minutes, then flip the fish over and continue to cook, partially covered, for a further 15 minutes. Remove the lid, increase the heat to high and cook, basting the fish with the caramel, for a final 8–10 minutes, until the caramel is reduced to a sticky sauce.

Transfer the fish to a serving dish, spoon over the caramel and top with the crispy pork lard, spring onion, crispy fried shallots and coriander. Finish with a drizzle of rendered pork fat over the fish and serve with steamed rice or salad.

Shelf Life

By Shannon Martinez,
Smith & Daughters

Cooking is faster, easier and more fun with a well-organised pantry. Follow these simple tips from the Smith & Daughters chef to bring some order to your kitchen, no matter how much space you have. With any luck, you'll never be caught short of ingredients again, nor lose a packet to the depths of a cupboard.

It's vital that a restaurant's dry store is properly organised so that anyone, regardless of whether they've worked there for a day or a decade, can find exactly what they need straight away. In restaurants we do everything for a reason, so it's worth looking into a similar system for your home. For ease of cooking and finding things, there has to be a method to the madness.

I clean out my pantry regularly, maybe once every two months. I'm an obsessive food-buyer – I have a problem – and I live alone. I don't need any more soy sauces or Shaoxing wines, but if I see a brand that looks amazing and I don't have it, I buy it. So I definitely have to go through my pantry. Even if you're not like me, it's worth regularly pulling everything out to get rid of stuff that's stale or you're just not using.

While you're doing that, put everything into labelled jars or tubs. Kmart has good jars. They're the same ones you get at Kitchen Warehouse, but at about a quarter of the cost. I wish I had a labeller. I stopped myself from getting one because I knew I'd get obsessive about it. I use masking tape and a marker, exactly like I would in a restaurant.

If you don't keep ingredients in identical jars, the things you always cook with are always in the front and you'll never use different ingredients. That's how people can get into a rut, cooking the same thing. If you walk into a pantry you want to get inspired, and think, "Oh, there's kombu there. Maybe I'll make something Japanese." That won't happen if you just see the same five or six things ahead of you.

I've also started using those food clips from Ikea. They're awesome. I'd never used them before and then when I moved into a new house there were some in the drawers. I couldn't believe how well they worked – I used to decant everything into a jar once it was opened because I didn't want things to go stale. These things actually keep chips crunchy. Now I'm really into those clips.

Everything should be organised into groups that make sense to you. My spices all sit on a single shelf, in identical jars. All my flours – plain, tipo 00, gluten free, rice flour – are in identical stackable tubs. All my pastas and noodles are in big, open-top pull-out tubs. Packets like that tend to get super messy otherwise.

For other packaged goods I have a shelf for Asian ingredients – vegan fish sauce, liquid kombu, a thousand different soy sauces. So if I'm making an Asian dish, it's easy. I just go to that section, and I know the thing I need is within that half a metre.

There's another shelf for European and Middle Eastern stuff – mustards, sauerkraut, harissa. Then there are separate spots for hot sauces, and for vinegars and condiments. All the canned foods go together in sub-groups like pulses, mushrooms, fruit and canned tomatoes. And there's another shelf for snacks.

Shopping in bulk at places like Costco, The Source and Terra Madre – any joint that you can fill up your own bags or jars – is cheap and saves on excess packaging. I do that and keep all the bulk stuff, like four-litre drums of oil, on my top shelves, while all the stuff I use regularly stays at eye level.

If you can adjust the height of your shelves, do it. I keep the clearance on my spice shelf super low, so the space doesn't go to waste. You can have another shelf for tall bottles, another for those big pull-out tubs and so on. Remember: method to the madness.

BAKED SALMON WITH TARATOR AND BURNT BUTTER
SHANE DELIA, MAHA

Prep time 15–20 minutes

Cook time 30 minutes

Serves 8

This is a real show stopper that has maximum impact when it hits the table. I love it because it's easy to put together. You buy the salmon boned so there's no filleting and you don't need to pan-fry it. So all the worries about cooking fish where people say, "Oh, I don't want to cook fish, it's a bit too hard," is alleviated. It's in the oven, then 20 minutes later it's out and it's done.

It's a glamorous-looking dish once the tahini and pomegranate and everything else is on it, too. I also like that it's easy to serve and eat. It's not like a chicken or a roast, where you have to carve it after it comes out of the oven.

Tarator is a tahini sauce, usually made with water and an acid, such as lemon or orange juice, and occasionally nuts. It's a big part of this dish, so make sure you put a lot on.

---

8 cloves garlic

2 preserved lemons skin only, chopped

1 tsp fennel seeds toasted

10g ginger peeled and chopped

2½ tbsp extra-virgin olive oil
plus extra for drizzling

Salt flakes I use Murray River salt flakes

1.2–1.3kg side of salmon pin-boned,
skinned and trimmed

TARATOR

150g tahini

Juice of 1 lemon

Juice of 1 orange

3 cloves garlic crushed

BURNT BUTTER

75g good-quality salted butter

50g pine nuts

50g chopped walnuts

1 tsp freshly ground coffee

1 clove garlic peeled and smashed

Juice of 1 lemon

Pomegranate tabouli see page 268,
to serve

Preheat the oven to 180°C.

Place the garlic, preserved lemon, fennel seeds and ginger in a mortar or food processor and pound or process, gently adding the olive oil, until you have a smooth paste. Taste and season with salt, then rub the mixture on both sides of the salmon.

Place the salmon on a large sheet of baking paper that will easily enclose the fish. Drizzle a little oil over the salmon and season with salt. Enclose the salmon in the baking paper, crumpling the edges to ensure no air can get out. Wrap in foil, then transfer to the oven and bake for 20–25 minutes (depending on the size of the fish), until just cooked through.

> I buy all my fish from Ocean Made in Collingwood. I've been going there for more than 20 years and I know it's all fresh. I like it when I go somewhere and I can watch them cut a side from the fish. Then I know it's really fresh, and it hasn't been rinsed, which takes away a lot of the good fatty flavour. Aussie salmon is really good, and so is New Zealand ora king salmon. It's a bit fattier and more luxurious. You can also use ocean trout, which is a really comparable fish.

To make the tarator, place the tahini in a large bowl. Slowly start adding the lemon juice, orange juice and then 50ml of water in a steady stream while whisking the tahini. The tahini will initially be firm and stiff, but will loosen as you add, the liquid. You should end up with a pouring consistency, so add a little more water if it's still thick. Stir through the garlic, then taste and season with salt.

→

Seafood

Baked salmon with tarator and burnt butter continued

I use Al Rabih, a tahini from Lebanon. But Australian tahini is great too – most of it is made using 100 per cent organic-certified sesame seeds, whereas some of the imported tahinis contain other ingredients such as peanuts.

Pour the tarator sauce into a large shallow serving dish. Remove the fish from the oven and carefully open the foil and paper, allowing the steam to release.

Gently place the fish on the tarator and cover with the tabouli.

To make the burnt butter, melt the butter in a small saucepan over medium heat. Add the nuts and cook, occasionally swirling the pan, for 2–3 minutes to slowly brown the butter. Add the coffee and garlic and continue to cook for another 1–2 minutes, until the butter is a rich nut brown and toasted. (Adding freshly ground coffee to burnt butter adds depth of flavour and results in a beautiful finish.) Add the lemon juice, then taste and season with salt. Using a slotted spoon, remove and discard the garlic.

Generously spoon the burnt butter over the fish and enjoy with friends.

Serve with my pomegranate tabouli on page 268.

Seafood

Korea World, Box Hill

"When you have guests at home, be organised. Cook as much as possible in advance. Don't try to overdo it and spend all your time in the kitchen. Your guests are coming to see you, not sit at the table waiting. So that's why you need to be organised, so you can chat and have fun."

TROTTOLE PASTA, PRAWNS, TOMATO AND TARRAGON
ANDREW MCCONNELL, TRADER HOUSE RESTAURANTS

Prep time 15 minutes

Cook time about 40 minutes

Serves 4

When I'm cooking at home on weekends, I can easily (and happily) spend the whole afternoon tinkering in the kitchen to make dinner. But mid-week it can be a bit of a balancing act to create maximum flavour in the shortest amount of time.

This is a dish I've been cooking for years. After paring down the process each time, I've worked out the quickest, most efficient way to make the sauce. Which, by the way, is concentrated and only a coating – the pasta shouldn't be swimming in it.

Texture plays a big part in how I cook, and this dish is no exception. Trottole pasta has a great bite and an almost chewy quality, perfectly complemented by the crunchy texture of the prawns.

---

6 whole raw tiger prawns 75–80g each

2 tbsp extra-virgin olive oil

1 brown onion finely diced

4 cloves garlic finely chopped

80ml (⅓ cup) white wine

4 large super-ripe tomatoes

400g trottole or another short-cut pasta, such as fusilli

Pinch of chilli flakes optional

1 tbsp salted butter

1 tbsp grated parmesan

¼ bunch tarragon leaves picked and chopped, plus extra to serve (optional)

Sea salt

Peel and devein the prawns, setting aside four prawn heads for the sauce. Chop the prawn meat and set aside in the fridge.

Heat the olive oil in a saucepan over low heat and gently cook the onion and prawn heads for 5 minutes (don't allow the onion to colour). Add the garlic and cook for 1–2 minutes, until fragrant. Add the white wine and simmer until it has evaporated.

Meanwhile, grate the tomatoes on the coarse side of a box grater. As you push the flesh and seeds through the grater, the skin will remain in one large piece, which you can then discard. Add the tomato pulp to the pan and simmer, stirring occasionally and gently pressing on the prawn heads to extract all the juices. Continue to cook for 30–35 minutes, gradually adding up to 125ml (½ cup) water so the sauce remains quite loose.

While the sauce is simmering, cook the pasta in a large saucepan of salted boiling water until al dente. Drain the pasta, reserving 250ml (1 cup) of the pasta cooking liquid.

Quickly remove and discard the prawn heads in the tomato sauce and add the pasta to the pan, along with the reserved prawn meat and chilli flakes (if using). Stir the prawn through the pasta for about 1 minute or until just cooked through. Remove from the heat and add a little of the reserved pasta cooking liquid if the pasta sauce seems a little dry.

Stir the butter, parmesan and tarragon leaves through the pasta, then season to taste with salt. Divide among shallow bowls and serve, garnished with a little more tarragon, if desired.

Seafood

CIOPPINO WITH MUSSELS AND ROCK FLATHEAD
COLIN MAINDS, CUTLER & CO.

Prep time 35 minutes

Cook time 2 hours

Serves 4–6

One of my oldest friends and mentors scored the job of a lifetime working for acclaimed chef Corey Lee at Benu in San Francisco. When I visited, I was blown away by how much the food drives the city's culture. It truly is the heart and soul of the place. Bayside, there are numerous harbour bistros all with their own version of cioppino, an Italian–American fish stew. I couldn't get enough of it and have been making it ever since.

A lot of people say cioppino is just an inferior version of bouillabaisse. I completely disagree. Cioppino is about using the best ingredients you can get hold of. It's versatile, fresh and balanced. I've always had a few secrets to enhancing the dish ... well, secret until now. One of the key parts to this recipe is using the normally discarded juice from the mussels and clams to create a "clamato" flavour. Bottled clamato (tomato and clam juice) is usually seasoned with added MSG. I like to add a sheet of kombu while reducing the broth to naturally enhance the umami.

Make this dish with the best-quality canned tomatoes you can find. It's so important to the finished flavour. I'm a snob for a good canned tomato and you will be too when you taste the difference. Look for DOP San Marzano tomatoes (Solania is my preferred brand).

1kg mussels scrubbed and debearded

250ml (1 cup) dry white wine

500g pipis soaked in cold water for 5 minutes, drained

100ml dry vermouth

80ml (⅓ cup) extra-virgin olive oil plus extra for drizzling

12 large raw prawns peeled and deveined, tails left intact, shells reserved

1 x 600g rock flathead cut into 3cm pieces (ask your fishmonger to fillet it and give you the large skeleton separately)

1 small sheet kombu

1 large golden shallot finely diced

1 small bulb fennel diced

2 cloves garlic finely sliced

Sea salt

1 tbsp tomato paste

→

Place a large saucepan over high heat, leaving it on the flame for a good few minutes. Add the mussels followed by the white wine, then cover and cook for about 1 minute, until the mussels just open. Strain the mussels in a colander set over a bowl to catch the liquid and set aside.

Wipe out the pan, then place it back over high heat. Once hot, add the pipis and vermouth and stir to combine. The pipis should open almost instantly. Strain over the mussels to again catch the liquid, then pour the liquid through a fine-meshed sieve to remove any grit. Pick the meat from half the mussels and pipis, leaving the other half in the shell.

> All the seafood can be substituted for what is fresh at the market. Melbourne has some of the best fish markets in Australia (South Melbourne, Prahran, Vic Market, Preston). Shop at the busiest stalls.

Heat 1 tbsp of the olive oil in a frying pan over medium heat and fry the prawn shells for about 8 minutes, until they turn a deep red. Add the rock flathead bone and kombu, then add the mussel and clam cooking liquid. Bring to the boil, then reduce the heat to a simmer and gently cook for 15–20 minutes until slightly reduced.

→

400g can good-quality peeled tomatoes

1 tbsp dried oregano or
2 tbsp fresh oregano leaves

2 strips lemon peel

2 strips orange peel

1 dried bay leaf

1 calamari hood cleaned and cut into bite-sized pieces

1 bunch flat-leaf parsley leaves picked and chopped

Sourdough to serve

Lemon wedges to serve

1 tsp Espelette pepper

Cioppino with mussels and rock flathead continued

Strain the liquid through a fine-meshed sieve into a bowl and discard the solids.

Place another large saucepan over medium heat, add the remaining 3 tbsp of oil, the shallot, fennel and garlic, along with a good pinch of salt, and cook for 5 minutes or until the fennel starts to soften. Try and avoid caramelising the vegetables by stirring often. Add the tomato paste and cook for 2 minutes, then add the strained seafood stock, canned tomatoes and 500ml (2 cups) of water. Bring to the boil, then add the oregano, lemon peel, orange peel and bay leaf. Reduce the heat to low and simmer for 45–60 minutes, until the broth has reduced by one-third and is slightly thickened. (Check the broth for seasoning as it reduces – I don't add much additional salt as the juice from the clams is salty.)

To finish the broth, add the rock flathead pieces and cook for 1 minute, then add the prawns and calamari followed by all the mussels and pipis. Stir gently.

Remove from the heat and scatter over most of the parsley leaves. Serve in deep bowls with torn sourdough bread and lemon wedges for squeezing over. Sprinkle over some Espelette pepper and extra parsley, then finish with a good drizzle of olive oil.

FISH COLLAR NABE
KOICHI MINAMISHIMA AND YOSHIKI TANO, MINAMISHIMA

Prep time 30 minutes
Cook time about 1 hour
Serves 4

At Minamishima, we buy in whole fish to fillet for our sushi, leaving the other parts of the fish, such as the fish collars, behind. One of my favourite ways to use this is in a fish collar nabe, which includes other pieces of fish and seafood not used for sushi in the restaurant.

This nabe (a dish cooked in an earthenware or cast-iron vessel; it's also the name of the pot) is similar to a fish stew, and is often part of our makanai (staff meal). We add rice and eggs to the soup to finish (we call this zosui), making it a meal on its own. It's particularly great with beer and nihonshu (sake).

500g fish collars or fillets snapper, coral trout and alfonsino work

500g wombok cut into large pieces

500g silken tofu cut into small pieces

1 small daikon peeled, cut in half lengthways and finely sliced

½ bunch spring onion cut into 5cm lengths

100g shiitake mushrooms stalks removed, halved

150g shimeji mushrooms ends removed, roughly chopped

½ bunch chrysanthemum greens leaves and tips picked

Sea salt

Shichimi togarashi to serve

Ponzu for dipping

DASHI
45g kombu
45g bonito flakes

SOUP BASE
3L dashi see above or use store-bought
135ml mirin
120ml good-quality light soy sauce
165ml sake

ZOSUI (RICE SOUP)
2 cups cooked short-grain rice
2 eggs lightly beaten
2 spring onions finely sliced

Bring a saucepan of water to the boil over high heat, then add the collars and cook for about 20 seconds. Immediately remove and rinse under cold running water to stop the cooking process. Using your fingers, carefully rub the fish on both sides to remove any remaining scales or blood, then cut into 5cm pieces and set aside.

> One of my favourite places to get fish is from Prahran Market. Ask the fishmonger to prepare the fish collars for you if they don't sell them.

If making dashi, combine 3.5L of room temperature water and the kombu in a large saucepan and allow to steep for 30 minutes. Set the pan over high heat and cook until bubbles start rising to the surface (about 70°C on a thermometer), then remove the kombu. Continue to heat the water until it reaches 80°C, then add the bonito flakes and cook until the thermometer reaches 85°C. Remove from the heat, wait for the bonito flakes to sink to the bottom of the pan, then strain through a fine-meshed sieve lined with a square of muslin over a large bowl. Do not press the bonito flakes as this will introduce unwanted flavours.

To make the soup base, place the dashi in a large clean saucepan, along with the remaining soup base ingredients. Bring to the boil over high heat, then add the fish collar, wombok, tofu, daikon, spring onion and both types of mushroom. Allow the mixture to return to the boil, then reduce the heat to a simmer and cook for 5 minutes. Stir through the chrysanthemum greens, then reduce the heat to low and cook for 2 minutes. Add ¼ tsp of sea salt or to taste.

Divide the mixture among four serving bowls, leaving 1.5L of soup in the pan to make zosui. Scatter a little shichimi togarashi over the top and serve with ponzu on the side for dipping.

To make the zosui, rinse the rice to remove excess starch, then reheat the soup in a saucepan over high heat. When the soup comes to the boil, stir through the cooked rice. Return the mixture to the boil, then slowly pour in the beaten egg and turn off the heat. Allow the egg to set, then serve, sprinkled with the spring onion.

Seafood

Dinner with the TT Racers

By James Cameron

The story of three friends, one pandemic, and the informal dinner club that helped them deal with it.

The thing about nicknames is, you never know what's going to stick. And when something does stick, it's already too late to change it. "TT Racers" is a ridiculous nickname for three friends who cook dinner together – we know that. But whenever I hear the term it always puts a smile on my face. I've embraced it. We all have.

The Racers are Magenta Burgin; me, James Cameron; and Nick Shelton, the founder of *Broadsheet*. Magenta drives an Audi TT and surely that means something, but how the name came to be is anybody's guess. Though we've been friends for a while, it was the pandemic that brought us together and solidified something between us. Cooking and eating really nice food is a whole lotta fun – that's a no-brainer – but the true surprise and gift of the time spent together was the support and love we gave one another through a difficult time. It became our world, and genuinely meant the world, too.

Each week goes something like this: Thursday – the messages start coming in like news flashes, "Guys! Rum baba! Let's do it." And like that we're off. Triggered by the memory of the rum baba at Carlton Wine Room, the menu starts to evolve, driven by what we've been missing, what's on our mind, what would work with this? Melbourne wine bar menu! Maybe some sardines? Or anchovies over whipped ricotta? We draw up market plans – who'll get what and where. The fun is in the process.

With tote bags full, ingredients are piled on the counter and loose timings set. We pat ourselves on the back for the handsome bounty before us. "Guys! How good is this?" We say "guys" a lot, as if the new season vegetables we've just sourced are the most important announcement of the day. At least in this little bubble and at this very moment, it is.

A little aperitivo breaks up the day; perhaps a few torn pieces of baguette with some freshly sliced prosciutto.

There's no single designated cook. Someone will just start. Or maybe a personal strength or affinity for a dish will dictate the day's chef, but this kitchen is democratic. Nick has become obsessed with the little tricks chefs use in their kitchens to make life easier (hence, this book), but one that has stuck is the use of tasting spoons. It's as simple as keeping a whole lot of teaspoons in a jar on your counter; we now reach for them intuitively both in absolute excitement, "GUYS! Try this!" or trepidation, "Guys, try this … "

The first meal, the icebreaker for the Racers, was whole salt-baked snapper. It's as impressive as it is easy (another quiet motto for the group); you make up the salt slurry and your beautiful snapper – cleaned by a fishmonger – just needs to be stuffed with simple flavourings, such as parsley, lemon and garlic. Fill it up, no need to season, you're about to cover it in two kilos of salt! Start laying it over, evenly building a little igloo for one. Press and smooth it around, put it in the oven and wait.

The salt acts like a defence against dryness, keeping all the moisture in and the fish tender. Make sure you scrape all the salt away, otherwise there's a strong chance it'll literally taste of the ocean. Gently lift it onto another plate, ideally placing it on a bed of something to your liking to keep it above any residual salt (we learned that the hard way). The Racers like to take three forks and dig in, but you can lift some nice pieces onto a plate and enjoy.

Things don't always go according to plan. "Happens," as Sydney-based Orazio D'Elia would say. We often watch Orazio cook on his Instagram Stories. His Italian cooking is the best; approachable and full of love and life. He posts everything, warts and all, and has become a kind of patron saint for the Racers. When something goes a little wrong, he'll just say "happens" and move on. We can't get enough of him, and have had our fair share of mishaps and "happens", too.

The wine we started buying during the pandemic has changed us forever. With no option to go out, every week our selections would up the ante. Champagne to start? But of course. Small producer with a witty backstory designed exactly to suck us in? Absolutely.

But it is the Italian wines that have really made the time pass. Like the Melbourne bars and restaurants we couldn't visit for so long, they stand in for destinations we still can't go to. We ruminate over the places we'll travel to when we can, as we pour whites from Alto Adige and reds from Sicily. Our excitement for what we will have next grows every week – just like the tab at the bottle shop. But the smiles win every time and saying no to the last bottle of Occhipinti on the shelf just wouldn't be right. That'd be very un-TT Racer. How could you explain yourself?

Over the months, we've enjoyed silly amounts of caprese salad and anchovies on ricotta. Magenta has been obsessed with chocolate nemesis and we've eaten whole cakes for eight. We've celebrated each other's birthdays with favourite dishes, tried to perfect the Martini and tarte tartin, always ready to impress when the time is right.

It's cliquey and borderline insufferable, but what tight knit group isn't? Eyes might roll, and I'm sure if you read the words "TT Racers" one more time, yours might too, but our tongues are firmly in our cheeks. We've been there for each other through an extraordinary time, but also for smaller things; difficult situations and issues that we have a go at trying to sort out.

SALT-BAKED SNAPPER
INSPIRED BY ORAZIO D'ELIA

Prep time 10 minutes | **Cook time** 30 minutes | **Serves** 4

Start with a snapper that's the size of a roasting pan or baking tray, about 1.2kg. Don't wash it. Just make sure it's clean, scaled and gutted.

We're a democratic kitchen, so if you're not on fish then you're on lemon (peeled and pip free) or garlic (sliced) or parsley (picked), ready to be stuffed inside. Put it all inside the cavity and place the fish on the baking tray.

Heat the oven to 230°C.

While this is going on, have someone mix the 2.5kg of rock salt with 250g of table salt and 250ml (1 cup) of water. Mix to a slurry and start loading the salt mix over the fish, spreading and patting evenly. The whole fish must be covered. If you're short on some salt here or there, it won't matter, you just want enough to cover the fish.

Bake in the oven for 30 minutes.

Once the time is up, take it out and let sit for a couple of minutes. Be warned, the salt gets very hot. So with a carving fork and something to tap it with, say a rolling pin or kitchen mallet, bang at the base of the fish and the salt should lift off in one or a few big chunks. Give the fish a brush and a quick clean. We found that by lifting the fish away to an awaiting platter, you'll get all of the great flavour of the bake, but not the overbearing taste of the salty brine.

Fillet or break into pieces and serve. Keep it simple. Eat with potatoes or a crisp leafy salad, and imagine you're at the beach.

YELLOW CURRY
BENJAMIN COOPER, CHIN CHIN

Prep time 40 minutes
Cook time 1 hour
Serves 6

If you come to my house for lunch there might be up to 15 dishes on the table. You end up taking a bit of each one, and all the sauces. When you're eating it all mixes together. It's like classic Malaysian or hawker street food – you're not eating an individual curry. You're eating everything and the flavours are all complementary.

I find yellow curry is the most versatile sauce and works well with meat, seafood and veggies. I like to put it in a big bowl with a ladle, for people to spoon over roasted chicken, prawns, eggplant or cauliflower, satay pumpkin or whatever other stuff I've made on the day.

I love chilli. I've spent some time cooking other cuisines over the years, and when I come back to Thai I'll occasionally bring a new ingredient into the fold. This recipe includes a Mexican chipotle chilli, which gives the sauce a subtle underlying smokiness that I find really appealing.

50g tamarind pulp
50ml boiling water
400ml can coconut cream
70ml vegetable oil
Pinch of sea salt
4–5 star anise
1–2 cinnamon quills
90g yellow curry paste see below
100g grated palm sugar
70–100ml soy sauce
1 tbsp yellow bean paste
625ml (2½ cups) coconut milk
250ml (1 cup) vegetable stock
or water
200g cherry tomatoes

YELLOW CURRY PASTE
12g (½ cup) large dried red chillies
80g piece of turmeric roughly chopped
5–6 cloves garlic roughly chopped
3–4 banana shallots roughly chopped
1 lemongrass stalk white and pale part
roughly chopped

→

Preheat the oven to 160°C fan-forced. Line a small roasting tin with baking paper.

To make the yellow curry paste, soak the dried chillies in a bowl of warm water for 15 minutes, then drain, slice open lengthways and remove the seeds. Place the chilli, turmeric, garlic, shallot, lemongrass and galangal in the prepared tin, add 125ml (½ cup) of water and roast for 20 minutes, until the water has evaporated. Gently toss the ingredients, then continue to roast for 5–10 minutes, until they smell fragrant and nutty. Remove from the oven and allow to cool a little, then transfer to a food processor or mortar and pestle and add the chipotle in adobo sauce and coriander roots. Blitz or pound to a smooth paste.

Next, rinse the spices separately under running water, then dry-toast them (also separately) in a small frying over medium heat for 1–2 minutes, until fragrant and completely dry.

Rinsing the spices allows them to reach a greater temperature when heated, without the risk of burning. Once they start to dry out, reduce the heat and continue to cook – you'll notice they release an incredible amount of fragrance. Genius!

Transfer the toasted spices to a mortar and pestle or spice grinder and pound or blitz to a fine powder. Add the spice mix and salt to the paste and set aside.

This recipe makes more curry paste than you'll need. Place the remaining paste in a zip-lock bag, squeeze out the air and freeze for 6–8 weeks.

→

40g piece of galangal peeled and roughly chopped

65g chipotle in adobo sauce roughly chopped

½ bunch coriander roots scraped clean

1½ tbsp coriander seeds

1 tbsp cumin seeds

1½ tbsp fennel seeds

1 small cassia quill

2 tsp sea salt

CHOICE OF PROTEIN

1.5–2kg roast pork belly so you get crispy crackling as well as juicy meat OR

1 whole roast chicken cut into portions OR

1kg prawns and crab for the photo we used blue swimmer crab cut into six pieces

TO SERVE

Crispy fried shallots

Thai basil leaves

Julienned makrut lime leaves

Rice

Adjard pickles see page 258

Yellow curry continued

Place the tamarind pulp in a heatproof bowl and pour over the boiling water. Set aside for 15–20 minutes to soften, then strain, reserving 2 tbsp of the tamarind juice.

Meanwhile, pour 250ml (1 cup) of the coconut cream into a heavy-based saucepan and set over medium–high heat. Add the oil, salt, star anise and cinnamon, then bring to the boil and cook for 5 minutes or until the cream starts to thicken and split. Add the curry paste, reduce the heat to medium and cook, stirring frequently.

Now, cooking curry is a complete sensory experience and I want you to use all your senses to achieve the best results. Once the curry paste starts to cook, the oil will separate out (the water will have evaporated) and the aromas will become really noticeable. Soon the paste will start to look like thick lava and darken in colour, and you'll begin to hear the paste start to fry. By this point, the aromas should be intoxicating – this is my favourite part! The aromas start to talk to you and tell you where the cook is at. Lower your face to the pan (making sure that it can't spit or burn you) and waft the aromas towards your nose. Close your eyes and smell (removing one sense can heighten another). What you smell is what you will taste.

The true depth of a curry sauce requires absolute focus on this part of the cook. Aromas are naturally released as moisture evaporates from each ingredient: the drier or hardier an ingredient, the longer it takes to cook out and for its aromas to escape. This means that a bright, zesty and punchy green curry will cook much faster than an earthy, fragrant, spice-laden red curry. The last thing you will smell is the dried spices. Once you can identify these aromas, usually after 10–15 minutes, you are ready for the next step.

Add the palm sugar and cook until the paste returns to the thick lava stage; it will smell nutty and sweet and the colour will have darkened considerably. Stir through the tamarind water, soy sauce, yellow bean paste, coconut milk and vegetable stock or water, then add your choice of protein and cook for 2–3 minutes, until warmed or cooked through. Finally, stir through the cherry tomatoes and check for seasoning.

Divide the curry among shallow bowls and top with crispy fried shallots, Thai basil leaves and julienned makrut lime leaves. Serve with rice and my adjard pickles on page 258.

Seafood

"I always cook my proteins separately to the curry. That way they actually taste like chicken or pork or whatever they are, and not just like curry."

Minh Phat, Abbotsford

NASI GORENG
RAPH RASHID, BEATBOX KITCHEN

Prep time 10 minutes
Cook time about 15 minutes
Serves 4

I grew up with this rice and I liked it, but I honestly pined for the lighter Cantonese version of fried rice. "Hey Pops, why's your nasi goreng deep in colour and funk? I want the one like at the Chinese takeaway!"

"You serious, young Snacc Boss? This is NASI GORENG from the village," my dad would say. "Now sit up and pierce that egg yolk with your fork and give it a hit of chilli or ketchup if you want." Ahh, my childhood. Smiley face.

550g (3 cups) just-cooked jasmine rice

4 cloves garlic

2 dried red chillies

2 tsp kapi Thai shrimp paste

130g peeled and deveined raw prawns cut into bite-sized pieces

160ml vegetable oil

40g small dried prawns or ikan bilis (dried anchovies)

50g banana shallot diced

2 tbsp kecap manis

1 tsp soy sauce

1 tsp fish sauce

1 spring onion cut into 1cm lengths

Good pinch of ground white pepper

1 tbsp chilli oil

ACCOMPANIMENTS

Sriracha or your favourite chilli sauce

4 fried eggs

Quick ginger see opposite

Lemon wedges

Crispy fried shallots

Spread the rice out on a tray and set aside to cool.

A lot of recipes call for day-old rice, which does work well. I use cooled rice for two reasons. First, I prefer my rice not dried-out or stale, which often happens in the fridge. Second, nasi goreng is not an afterthought; I'm not just using left-over rice. I want to blast it pretty much straight from the pan when I'm hungry. So I like to dry out the exterior of the rice, while keeping the inside tender. It'll still be a bit sticky and that's cool – you just don't want it too wet.

Meanwhile, pound the garlic, chilli and shrimp paste using a mortar and pestle until you have a smooth paste. It will get fragrant!

Bring a saucepan of water to the boil . Add the chopped prawns and blanch for 1–2 minutes, until tender. Drain and set aside. I like to cook the prawn separately instead of cooking it with the rice, so it doesn't release extra moisture into the dish.

Heat 100ml of the oil in a wok over medium heat, then add the dried prawns or ikan bilis and fry for 2–3 minutes, until crisp. Transfer to paper towel to drain.

Clean and wipe dry the wok, then add the remaining oil and set over low heat. Add the garlic paste and cook for 2 minutes, breaking up the mixture with a wooden spoon as it cooks. Add the shallot and cook for another minute, then add the cooled rice and increase the heat to medium–high, stirring to coat the rice grains in the paste. Continue to toast the rice for 2–3 minutes, then add the sauces and spring onion. Stir and flip and stir and scrape up and down the wok.

Add the blanched prawn and dried prawns or ikan bilis and continue the wok shuffle for a few seconds. Remove the wok from the heat and add a good hit of white pepper and chilli oil. Stir through and serve with your choice of accompaniments.

To make the quick ginger, pound a 2cm piece of ginger, 1 spring onion and a pinch of salt using a mortar and pestle until smooth. Balance with a splash of vinegar to taste, then spoon it over the rice.

Seafood

"I like to choose which mouthfuls get
the sauce, hence why I serve it on the side."

POULT
& MEA

RY
T

Poultry & Meat

KYUSHU-STYLE CHASHU TONKOTSU RAMEN
ROYSTAN LEOW, MR RAMEN SAN

Prep time 3 hours

Cook time 3 hours 30 minutes, plus 2–12 hours marinating

Serves 4

I've been making ramen professionally for more than 10 years, and for the last few years many of my customers have been asking me how to make ramen at home, especially Kyushu-style tonkotsu ramen. Not to be confused with tonkatsu (breaded, deep-fried pork cutlet), tonkotsu loosely translates to "pork bone soup", and chashu is braised pork.

Making a restaurant-quality tonkotsu ramen takes a very long time (usually 2–3 days), as most of the elements are prepared from scratch, including the hand-made ramen noodles. Additionally, some of the ingredients that we use at Mr Ramen San are often difficult to source, even at an Asian grocer. Not to mention the huge pots and pans we use to cook our soups.

Over the years, I have developed easier home-cooked ramen recipes that are almost as good as what comes out of a professional kitchen, using simple equipment and ingredients that you can get from your local supermarkets or your nearest Asian grocer. (You will need a pressure cooker for this recipe.)

Here, I would like to introduce an easy Kyushu-style tonkotsu ramen recipe for home. You can make it over a weekend. There are five basic elements to ramen: noodles, tare (sauce), broth, toppings and seasoned oil. The broth, toppings and oil can be stored in the fridge for a few days, so don't worry if you can't finish making them in a single day.

400g fresh noodles such as Chinese yangchun or egg noodles

Bunch of spring onions finely sliced

1 long red chilli finely sliced (optional)

1 tbsp finely chopped garlic

CHASHU TOPPING

500g rindless pork belly

250ml (1 cup) shoyu

40ml white wine

80g caster sugar

EGG TOPPING

4 large eggs at room temperature

70ml shoyu

2½ tbsp mirin

→

To make the chashu topping, fill a large stockpot with water and bring to the boil over high heat. Add the pork belly and return to the boil, then reduce the heat to a simmer and cook for 60–80 minutes, until you can pierce the flesh with a skewer and it comes out clean. Remove the pork belly and reserve the water.

Wash the pork belly under cold running water, then place in a large zip-lock back with the shoyu, white wine and sugar. Leave to marinate for 2–12 hours (the longer you leave it, the better the flavour will be). Once marinated, cut the chashu into thin slices.

To make the egg topping, bring a saucepan of water to a vigorous boil over high heat. Pierce the end of each egg with a needle (this prevents them from cracking when they hit the water), then add to the pan and boil for exactly 6.5 minutes. Remove using a slotted spoon and transfer to an ice bath. Set aside for 15 minutes, then peel.

Place the peeled eggs in a zip-lock bag with the shoyu, mirin and 3 tbsp of water. Set aside in the fridge to marinate for 2 hours.

→

Korea World, Box Hill

TONKOTSU BROTH

1kg pork back bones ask your butcher to chop them into smaller pieces

1kg pork knuckle bones

350g chicken carcass or bones

20g kombu

100g peeled and diced potatoes

TARE

20g dried fish such as anchovies

1 dried shiitake mushroom

5cm square piece of kombu

20g Himalayan pink salt or sea salt

1 tsp mirin or ¼ tsp honey

SEASONED OIL

375ml (1½ cups) vegetable oil

3 tbsp sliced garlic

Kyushu-style chashu tonkotsu ramen continued

To make the broth, place all the pork bones in a large stockpot and add enough water to cover. Boil the bones for about 10 minutes, until they turn brown and no more blood comes out.

In a separate saucepan, blanch the chicken bones in boiling water for 10 minutes.

Drain all the bones and rinse under cold running water to remove all the remaining impurities and scum.

Put the bones, kombu, potato and 2.7L of the reserved pork belly water in a pressure cooker. Don't put the lid on yet. Wait until the water starts to boil, then discard the kombu. Seal the cooker and turn to high heat and high pressure. Cook for 35 minutes, then turn off the heat to release the pressure. Remove the lid according to the manufacturer's instructions, then turn to high heat again and stir the soup constantly for about 10 minutes. (The colour of the broth may not be as white and creamy as professional tonkotsu broth, but the depth of flavour will be almost the same.)

To make the tare, place the dried fish, shiitake mushroom and kombu in a food processor and blitz to a powder. Transfer to a small saucepan with 500ml (2 cups) of water and place over medium heat. Simmer for 5 minutes, then strain the liquid through a square of muslin or a coffee filter into a bowl. Add the salt and mirin or honey and stir until the salt dissolves.

> The more varieties of dried fish you use, the more complex and flavoursome your tare will be. If you're pushed for time, replace the tare with 2 tbsp shiro dashi per person, available at Asian grocers.

To make the seasoned oil, place the oil in a saucepan over medium heat and add the garlic. Cook for 10 minutes or until the garlic is golden brown, then remove from the heat and strain the oil into a clean container. Discard the garlic.

Cook the noodles according to the packet instructions, then drain and divide among four deep serving bowls. To assemble the ramen, add the following to each bowl: 2 tbsp of tare, 1 tbsp of seasoned oil, 350ml boiling tonkotsu broth, some sliced chashu and an egg, sliced in half. Finish with spring onion, chilli (if using) and garlic, to taste.

"Make it fun, make it relaxed. Study and learn, but do it all at your own pace – don't bite off more than you can chew. It's got to be enjoyable, because that's the foundation of cooking. So do what you have to do to make it enjoyable, and immerse yourself in that."

BEEF PHO
NAM NGUYEN, GOOD DAYS

Prep time 1 hour 30 minutes

Cook time 6 hours 30 minutes

Serves 6

It's interesting that all over Australia you find the same variations of pho, largely because the Vietnamese community who first migrated here in the '70s and '80s were all from the south. My trips to Vietnam have really expanded my concept and definition of Vietnamese food from what I grew up eating in suburban Adelaide. With pho, for example, the flavours and ingredients differ so much between regions. From the broth – which can be dark and rich or sometimes light – to the condiments and herbs, and even down to the grade and cuts of beef.

When opening Good Days in 2016, I wanted to offer my take on Vietnamese food. We'd seen the popularity of banh mi taken to another level by modern interpretations, but not pho. I was able to marry my appreciation of Japanese cooking with Vietnamese flavours, and the art of a good ramen formed the foundation of our beef pho – it's punchy and full-bodied, and uses a lot more fat than is traditional.

The quality and range of fresh ingredients sets our pho apart, but all pho requires hours of careful cooking. Many people are accustomed to paying as little as $12 for a bowl. I hope when you read this recipe, it will shed some light on the complexity of the dish and the skill and care that goes into it.

500g eye fillet steak cheaper cuts such as topside also work well

Sea salt and freshly ground black pepper

2 tsp vegetable oil

BROTH

2.5kg beef bones

1kg beef brisket

2 brown onions unpeeled, cut in half

1 red onion unpeeled, cut in half

110g piece of ginger unpeeled, cut in half

1 small cassia bark or cinnamon quill

8 star anise

2 cardamom pods

3 tsp coriander seeds

1 heaped tsp cloves

→

Season the eye fillet generously with salt and pepper. Heat the oil in a heavy-based frying pan over high heat, then add the eye fillet and sear on all sides for 8–10 minutes, until a crust forms (you just want to sear the outside, so that when you slice it later the beef will have a nice dark brown ring around the edge). Remove the fillet from the pan and set aside to cool, then place in the freezer. This will make slicing easier.

To make the broth, bring a large stockpot of water to the boil over high heat. Add the beef bones and boil for 5 minutes, then drain. Wash the bones thoroughly to remove any scum and clean the pot.

Place the cleaned bones back in the pot and place the brisket on top. Add enough water to cover the bones and brisket by 5cm, then place over medium–low heat and very slowly bring to the boil. This should take 1–2 hours.

Line a fine-meshed sieve with muslin or a clean Chux cloth and set over a bowl. Using a ladle, skim any scum that forms on top of the broth into the sieve. This allows you to separate the beef fat (tallow) from the scum. You'll need that beef fat later. Adjust the heat to a very gentle simmer, then cook for 4 hours, skimming the surface as soon as any scum rises to the top.

→

BOX HILL ASIAN FOOD CE

562
Station St. Box Hill

International Calls **0**

Lyca mobile

LETTUCE

CUCKOO
CUCKOO
CUCKOO

"Try and source a variety of bones: oxtail, chuck, bone marrow and knuckle will give your broth more complexity, with the knuckle and bone marrow helping to thicken the broth resulting in good mouthfeel. It's a good idea to write down the ratio of bones used every time you cook beef pho. If you cook it enough, you'll establish a golden ratio that works for you."

50g rock sugar

120ml fish sauce we use
Three Crabs Brand

1 tsp dry mushroom seasoning
an umami bomb that replaces MSG;
available at Asian grocers

2 tbsp sea salt

PICKLED GARLIC

100ml white vinegar

50g raw sugar

4 cloves garlic finely sliced

TO SERVE

600g fresh pho noodles

500g bean sprouts

Bunch of Thai basil

Lemon wedges

Hoisin sauce

2 spring onions finely sliced

½ bunch of coriander leaves picked
and roughly chopped

½ red onion finely sliced

Beef pho continued

Remove the brisket and set aside to cool, then place in the fridge. Increase the heat to medium–high and boil the broth for a further 1–2 hours, continuing to skim the surface and topping up with water to ensure the bones remain submerged. This extra cooking allows the knuckles to break down and release their collagen. (We crank the heat to give our pho more body and to pump the beefiness of the broth. This veers it towards the technique used to make ramen broth.)

Preheat the grill to high, then grill the brown and red onion and ginger for 10 minutes, turning often, until slightly charred. Set aside.

Meanwhile, to make the pickled garlic, combine the vinegar, sugar and 200ml of water in a small bowl. Stir until the sugar dissolves, then add the garlic and set aside for 2 hours to pickle.

Reduce the broth to a gentle boil and add the charred onion and ginger. Cook for a further 1 hour.

Next, dry toast the cassia bark or cinnamon, star anise and cardamom pods in a frying pan over medium heat for 5 minutes, until lightly coloured, then add the coriander seeds and cloves and continue to cook until the spices are evenly toasted. Transfer to a muslin cloth and tie with a knot to secure.

Remove the broth from the heat and add the spice mix, ensuring it is completely submerged. Cover and set aside for 1 hour for the spices to steep.

At this point, remove the noodles from the fridge. Gently separate them as best you can (don't worry too much, as they'll separate further upon cooking).

Strain the broth through a large square of muslin set over a large heatproof bowl. Return the broth to a clean pan and discard the solids. Bring it to a gentle simmer over medium–low heat and add the rock sugar, fish sauce, mushroom seasoning and salt. Skim any scum that rises to the top again.

Now it's time to taste. You want your broth to be a balance of sweet, salty and umami. Every broth you make will be different so you need to adjust the seasoning accordingly. Your broth should be slightly over-seasoned to accommodate the noodles and beef. Once you are happy with the seasoning, your broth is ready.

To assemble the pho, slice the brisket into 5mm thick slices. Slice the eye fillet as thinly as you can. Divide the bean sprouts, Thai basil and lemon wedges among six serving plates and pour a small quantity of hoisin sauce into six dipping bowls.

Bring a saucepan of water to a gentle boil over medium heat, then add the noodles and cook, stirring to prevent them from clumping, for 30 seconds or until soft and separated. Drain and divide among six deep serving bowls.

Spoon 1 tbsp of the reserved beef fat (tallow) into each bowl and top with a few slices of the pickled garlic. Place the brisket and eye fillet on top of the noodles, then ladle over the hot broth to warm through the beef. Finish with the spring onion, coriander and red onion, and serve with the bean sprout plates and hoisin dipping bowls on the side.

BOAT NOODLES
CHAVALIT PIYAPHANEE, SOI 38

Prep time 1 hour
Cook time 5 hours
Serves 4

These noodles got their name because they were originally sold from boat vendors. The boats would rock backwards and forwards and side to side. The vendors didn't want the soup to spill, so they packed a lot of flavour into a minimal amount of broth.

I've been eating boat noodles since I was a little kid, growing up in Bangkok. My first time was at a vendor called Nai Buem Kuay Teow, next door to my primary school, when I was five or six. It's been there for ages. And it's funny, because it turns out that my business partner, Andy Buchan, tried boat noodles there for the first time, too.

After I moved to Australia in 1997, I opened Thai restaurants – normal, standard Thai restaurants where we just served pad thai and all that. Andy was a regular customer who would eat everything on the menu. Eventually, he approached me because he'd found a space and wanted to open a boat noodle shop with me. So we took a trip back to that same vendor in Bangkok and ate boat noodles together, returning again and again until we'd recreated the recipe.

At the beginning, I didn't think Soi 38 would work. I didn't think people would understand boat noodles and why the dish didn't have much broth – but it turns out that they could. It's a good feeling when people agree with the food you like.

500g beef intercostals, oyster blade or gravy beef cut into bite-sized pieces

100ml fish sauce

60g sugar

2 coriander roots scrubbed clean and bruised using the side of a knife

2.5cm piece of ginger sliced

200g eye fillet

BOAT NOODLE BROTH

7–8 long green chillies

1 bulb garlic unpeeled, sliced in half horizontally

1½ tbsp coriander seeds

1 cinnamon quill

5 star anise

8g Sichuan peppercorns

1.5kg pork back bones

100ml kecap manis

→

Place 1.5L of water in a large saucepan and bring to the boil over high heat. Add the beef, fish sauce, sugar, coriander roots and ginger, then cover, reduce the heat to a simmer and cook for 2 hours or until the beef can be easily shredded with a fork. Remove from the heat and set aside.

Meanwhile, to make the broth, place 5L of water in a large stockpot and bring to the boil over high heat.

Place the green chillies, garlic, coriander seeds, cinnamon, star anise and Sichuan peppercorns in a dry frying pan and toast over medium heat for 5 minutes, until fragrant. Remove from the heat and set aside.

Add the pork back bones to the boiling water, then stir through the toasted ingredients. Add the remaining broth ingredients except the coconut milk, then reduce the heat to medium and simmer for 2 hours. At the end of the cooking time, bring the broth to the boil and stir through the coconut milk.

Meanwhile, to make the crispy pork and garlic oil, place a frying pan over high heat and add the fat and salt. Saute for 10 minutes or until rendered and crispy.

→

Poultry & Meat

75ml light soy sauce

50ml garlic pickle juice
look for this at Asian grocers

50g soybean paste

50ml Shaoxing rice wine

40g brown sugar

2 tbsp sea salt

20g rock sugar

2cm piece of ginger sliced

2cm piece of galangal sliced

2 pandan leaves

2 coriander roots scrubbed clean
and bruised using the side of a knife

250ml (1 cup) coconut milk

PORK AND GARLIC OIL

300g pork back fat coarsely diced

1 tbsp sea salt

2 bulbs garlic cloves finely sliced

TO SERVE (per person)

150g noodles of your choice

50g morning glory cut into
3cm lengths

Handful of bean sprouts

Handful of coriander leaves

¼ bunch of sawtooth coriander

Boat noodles continued

Reduce the heat to medium and add the garlic, then stir for 5 minutes or until the garlic is soft. Remove from the heat and set aside. (We remove the pan from the heat before the garlic starts to colour because the residual heat in the fat will continue to cook it.)

Sear the eye fillet in a frying pan over medium–high heat on all sides for 10 minutes or until a crust has formed. Set aside to rest for 5 minutes, then slice thinly.

To serve, cook the noodles and morning glory in boiling water to your preferred softness, then drain and divide among deep serving bowls. Drizzle over 1 tbsp of drained pork and garlic oil (keep the crispy bits for the topping) and toss to combine and prevent the noodles from sticking.

Place the eye fillet and slow-cooked beef on top of the noodles, then pour the boiling broth over the top. Finish with a small amount of bean sprouts, coriander leaves and sawtooth coriander, along with a little of the crispy fat and garlic from the pork and garlic oil (don't add any extra oil at this stage). Serve immediately.

> Boat noodles usually contains cow's blood, but we use coconut milk instead. We thought blood might freak people out. If you do want to add it, it makes the broth richer. Put in it each bowl before you serve the noodles – 1 tbsp of blood per ladle of broth.

Poultry & Meat

FETTUCCINE BOLOGNESE
GUY GROSSI, GROSSI FLORENTINO

Prep time 25 minutes
Cook time 1 hour 30 minutes–2 hours
Serves 6

This is our traditional recipe for bolognese that I have eaten since I was a kid; it's how Mum made it for me. We use a mixture of mince to provide richness and depth of flavour, but you can use just beef if you prefer. We also add red wine, but if you prefer a lighter-style ragu you can use white wine, stock or even water – you just need to make sure that you simmer it slowly to develop the flavour and texture.

In general, a ragu should be cooked over low heat using cuts of meat, such as shoulder or mince, that lend themselves to slow cooking, but if you do need to reduce the ragu more quickly, simply add a little paste made from flour and water, just to give it that extra boost.

In terms of spice, we use nutmeg and clove, which add another dimension without overpowering the dish, but feel free to use more or less depending on your taste. The rest is really about pairing the meat with herbs and a liquid that suits. There's nothing like the smell of a ragu cooking on the stove to make you feel good inside – it's comfort food at its best.

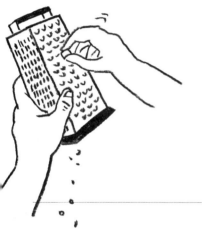

100ml olive oil

1 large brown onion finely chopped

2 cloves garlic finely chopped

800g good-quality beef mince

100g good-quality pork mince

100g good-quality chicken mince

1 tsp finely chopped long red chilli

1 tsp finely chopped sage leaves

½ cup chopped flat-leaf parsley leaves

1 dried bay leaf

Pinch of ground cloves

½ nutmeg finely grated

Sea salt and freshly ground black pepper

300g tomato paste

200ml red wine

500g home-made or good-quality store-bought fettuccine

200g Parmigiano Reggiano grated

Heat the olive oil in a large saucepan over medium heat, add the onion and garlic and cook for 4–5 minutes, until softened. Add all the mince and cook, stirring constantly, for 8–10 minutes, until well browned, breaking up any large lumps with the back of a wooden spoon.

Stir in the chilli, herbs and spices and season generously with salt and pepper. Add the tomato paste and cook for 2 minutes, then pour in the wine and simmer for about 2 minutes, until reduced by half. Add 1L of water and mix well for 2 minutes, then bring to the boil.

Reduce the heat to a simmer and gently cook for 1–1.5 hours, until the bolognese is reduced and thick. Season to taste with salt and pepper.

Bring a large saucepan of salted water to the boil, add the fettuccine and give it a gentle stir so the pasta doesn't stick together. Cook for 5–6 minutes, until al dente.

Drain the fettuccine and stir it through the bolognese until well coated. Serve with a generous sprinkling of grated Parmigiano.

Whenever the Valmorbida family gets together, there's usually pasta involved. Nothing is planned, necessarily. But the ingredients are always in the pantry. It's been this way for decades.

"You'd wake up on the weekend, it'd be quite late, and Dad would be in the kitchen making pasta," says Lisa Valmorbida, who runs Lygon Street gelateria Pidapipó and its counterparts in Windsor, Fitzroy and the CBD.

Next door, her brother Jamie and cousin Luca Sbardella own King & Godfree, the Italian grocery store founded by their grandfather Carlo and his brothers in the 1950s. The family has been involved with food for 70 years, through brands such as Moro olive oil, Val Verde tomatoes and Sirena Tuna.

Lisa and Jamie's sister, Amanda, lives in Sydney. When she's down, the three siblings and their cousin usually catch up to eat.

"When we're all together we cook pasta a lot, and friends will be around. It's often a late-night thing, when we're a bit hungry after being out. We all learned from Dad, but have our own styles.

"There's this idea that fresh pasta is better than dried pasta. I don't agree. I think there's a place for both of them. If we're making lasagne or pappardelle with ragu, that's when we'd use fresh. And my grandma Elsie used to make gnocchi, so that's something that's been passed down. But we use dried pasta the most frequently."

"When we're all together we cook pasta a lot, and friends will be around. It's often a late-night thing, when we're a bit hungry after being out. We all learned from Dad, but have our own styles."

On this afternoon Jamie and Lisa made:

PACCHERI, TOMATO AND ITALIAN SAUSAGE
JAMIE VALMORBIDA

Prep time 10 minutes | **Cook time** 30 minutes | **Serves** 6

600g Italian pork sausages
3 tbsp extra-virgin olive oil
3 cloves garlic finely chopped
1 red onion finely chopped
90g (⅓ cup) tomato paste
3 tbsp dry white wine
2 x 400g cans peeled tomatoes
1 tsp chilli flakes
2 pinches of sugar
Salt and pepper
500g paccheri
2 tbsp butter
100g (1 cup) grated Parmigiano Reggiano

Squeeze the sausage meat out of the skins and chop into small chunks. Add half the oil to a large frying pan and begin browning the meat over medium–high heat. Once browned, turn off the heat and set aside.

Add the remaining oil and the garlic to another large frying pan and cook over low heat for 2 minutes. Add the onion and cook for 2 minutes. Add the tomato paste and cook, stirring, for about 4 minutes, until it has caramelised. Add the white wine and cook, stirring constantly, for about 3 minutes, until the liquid has mostly evaporated.

Add the canned tomatoes, chilli flakes, sugar, salt and pepper to taste, and the cooked sausage. Turn up the heat and bring to a boil, then reduce to medium–low heat and cook for 20 minutes.

Meanwhile, fill a large saucepan with water and salt the water so it tastes like sea water. Bring to a rapid boil and cook the paccheri for about 1 minute less than the packet instructions, timing it to finish at the same time as the sauce. Drain, reserving 250ml (1 cup) of pasta water.

Transfer the paccheri to the pan with the sauce. Cook, stirring constantly and adding ¼ cup of pasta water at a time as needed. Add the butter and most of the Parmigiano, continuing to stir, until a thick, glossy sauce forms.

Divide among bowls, then top with more Parmigiano.

LINGUINE, SEA URCHIN, TOMATO AND PARSLEY
LISA VALMORBIDA

Prep time 10 minutes | **Cook time** 20 minutes | **Serves** 4

3 tbsp extra-virgin olive oil
plus extra to finish
4 cloves garlic finely chopped
½–1 red chilli finely chopped
200g fresh cherry tomatoes finely chopped
125ml (½ cup) dry white wine
500g linguine
200g sea urchin
1 bunch parsley leaves picked
and finely chopped

Fill a large saucepan with water. Salt the water so it tastes like sea water and bring to a rapid boil.

Add the oil, garlic and chilli to a large saucepan or deep frying pan and cook over medium heat for about 3 minutes, until fragrant.

Add the tomatoes and cook for 5 minutes, until they start to break down into a sauce. Add the white wine and cook for 2 minutes.

Add the pasta to the boiling water while you continue cooking the tomatoes down. If the pan starts to dry out, add some pasta water from the boiling pot. You want to finish cooking the pasta in the sauce, so it's important to taste the pasta and take it out once it's al dente. If the packet says to cook for 10 minutes, I would recommend taking it out at 7 minutes.

Just before the pasta is ready, add the sea urchin to the sauce and break it up with a wooden spoon. It will break up into the sauce as it cooks.

Once the pasta is al dente, turn off the heat. Using tongs, transfer the pasta to the sauce. Allow the pasta to finish cooking in the sauce, stirring constantly and adding ¼ cup of pasta water at a time as needed, until a thick sauce forms.

Once the pasta is cooked, turn off the heat, add the chopped parsley and finish with some good-quality extra-virgin olive oil.

"The quality of your ingredients is essential, and your choice of canned tomatoes is everything – San Marzano all the way! Why? Because of their sweetness, delicate flavour, balance of acidity and consistency in quality."

LASAGNE
JOEY KELLOCK, 1800 LASAGNE

Prep time about 1 hour
Cook time about 5 hours 30 minutes
Serves 12

This is essentially my first ever lasagne recipe. That's why I call it the Carlton recipe: I was living in Carlton and I did a bunch of lasagnes for a friend's dinner party – and that's pretty much what started 1800 Lasagne.

When I make lasagne, I focus equally on each element as I'm going through the building, cooking and preparation process. Each element is special, and you need to treat it as such. It's a lot of seasoning, it's putting cheese in all the right places and it's making your ragu specifically for lasagne, not just taking a bolognese sauce and whacking it between some sheets of pasta.

The difference between an average lasagne, a good lasagne and a great lasagne is really going the extra mile. That's why sometimes when you order lasagne at a restaurant it doesn't meet your expectations – because they've cut corners. And you can't really cut corners with a great lasagne.

400g firm mozzarella shredded
250g Grana Padano grated
400g fresh pasta sheets

NAPOLI SAUCE
120ml extra-virgin olive oil
½ brown onion cut through the root
6 large cloves garlic peeled and smashed
4–6 basil leaves
Sea salt
3 x 400g cans San Marzano tomatoes
Brown sugar to taste (optional)

RAGU
80ml (⅓ cup) extra-virgin olive oil
250g pork mince
1kg veal mince
500g pork and fennel sausages casings removed
125g flat pancetta finely diced
125g mild cacciatore salami casing removed, finely diced
1 large brown onion finely diced
4 large celery stalks stringy bits removed, finely diced

→

Making a lasagne is a labour of love, so put on some music and pour yourself a glass of wine. Be the lasagne.

To make the napoli sauce, place a saucepan over medium–low heat and add the olive oil and onion, cut side down. Gently bring the oil up to heat – we're trying to infuse as much onion flavour into the oil as possible. Cook for about 8 minutes, until the onion starts to sizzle and has a bit of colour, then add the garlic, basil and 1 tsp of salt, reduce the heat to low and gently cook for 6–7 minutes, until the garlic just starts to colour. Add the San Marzano tomatoes (use an old knife to chop them up while they're still in their cans or break them up in the saucepan) and stir through. Swill out the cans with 250ml (1 cup) of water and add to the pan. Bring up to a gentle simmer, then cook, stirring frequently, over low heat for 30 minutes or until slightly thickened. Remove and discard the onion, then taste and season with salt and, depending on your canned tomatoes, a little brown sugar.

Meanwhile, to make the ragu, pour the oil into a large saucepan and set over medium–high heat. Working in three separate batches, brown the pork mince, veal mince and sausage for 8–10 minutes each batch, breaking up the mince with the back of a wooden spoon. Set the browned mince and sausage aside, then add the pancetta and cacciatore to the pan and cook for 6–7 minutes, until they've released their delicious juices and the fat has rendered. Using a slotted spoon, set aside with the mince and sausage.

→

Lasagne continued

1 large carrot finely diced

6 cloves garlic peeled and smashed

1 tbsp Sicilian dried oregano

500ml (2 cups) white wine

250ml (1 cup) red wine

2 fresh bay leaves

750ml (3 cups) stock I use veal, but you can use a mixture of chicken and beef

Salt flakes and ground white pepper

BECHAMEL

1.5L full-cream milk

150g unsalted butter

150g (1 cup) plain flour

70g Grana Padano grated

Salt flakes and ground white pepper

I buy my meat from Donati's Fine Meats on Lygon Street. Go there for the Puccini soundtrack and the beautiful flowers from Mrs Donati's garden, stay for the finest meats in Melbourne. If you don't have a favoured butcher, then find one, and go there often.

Don't eat meat? No worries! Grab 1.5kg of eggplant and cut lengthways into 5–10mm thick slices. Salt both sides of the eggplant and set aside in a colander for 15 minutes to remove any bitterness and excess liquid. Shake off the excess salt and pat dry with paper towel. Brush the eggplant with olive oil and place on baking trays lined with baking paper in single layers. Bake in a 175°C oven for 15 minutes or until you start to notice a bit of colour, then use in place of the ragu.

Add the onion, celery, carrot, smashed garlic and oregano to the pan, reduce the heat to medium and cook for 6–8 minutes, until the vegetables are soft and beginning to caramelise. Add the wine and stir to deglaze the pan, then cook for 8–10 minutes, until reduced.

This soffritto is so important. It is the base of your lasagne – the foundation of the house. If your onion isn't translucent and you're not getting deposits of caramelisation in the pan, it means you're going to have a bland base that won't deglaze properly. So basically, don't mess with the soffritto. Put the time in and start off on the right foot.

I like to use dried Sicilian oregano. Why? Take a look at a photo of Sicily and tell me you don't want your oregano from there! Also, bay leaves need to be fresh. There are heaps of trees around Melbourne, just ask permission before helping yourself.

Return all the meat to the pan, along with the bay leaves, stock and napoli sauce. Allow the mixture to come to a gentle simmer, then reduce the heat to low and cook with the lid ajar and stirring frequently, for 2.5 hours or until reduced and thick. Season with salt and white pepper to taste, then remove from the heat and set aside.

I like veal stock here as it's lighter than beef but stronger than chicken. It's just in between and because we're already rolling with a pretty pork-heavy meat sauce, the veal stock pulls the lasagne away from that white-meat chicken-pork vibe. I'm never at home enough to make my own stock, so it's store-bought all the way. I buy my stocks from Piedimonte's in Fitzroy North because they have heaps to choose from.

To make the bechamel, pour the milk into a saucepan and set over low heat to gently warm through. Melt the butter in a separate large saucepan over medium–low heat and add the flour. Stirring constantly (I use a heatproof spatula so the flour doesn't catch), cook out the flour for about 5 minutes, until it looks sexy. Add the warm milk, 250ml (1 cup) at a time, whisking vigorously after each addition, until all the milk is incorporated and the sauce is smooth.

Switch back to your spatula, increase the heat to medium and continue to cook, stirring frequently, until the bechamel is slightly thickened and the taste of raw flour has gone. The whole process should take around 30 minutes.

Whisk in the cheese and season with salt and white pepper (don't be too heavy-handed with the seasoning, as we want the bechamel to be delicate and clean-tasting). Set aside, covered to keep warm.

Preheat the oven to 180°C.

To build the lasagne, bring a large saucepan of heavily salted water to the boil. Grab a large baking dish (mine measures 33cm x 26cm x 8cm) and set up your ingredients in a production line ready to go.

> As a little secret, when I'm making ragu, I skim the fat off the top of the ragu and then I set it aside and kind of let it congeal a little bit. And then, before I start the building process, once that fat is congealed – deep-red ragu fat – I get a basting brush and I paint the whole inside of the baking dish with that fat. Then I get handfuls of Grana Padano and flare it out in the dish so it sticks to the sides and base. Then – and only then – do I start building the lasagne. This step creates a cheese and ragu-fat crust on the lasagne as it cooks and sizzles. That is one of the hottest lasagne tips you'll ever have in your life, I'll tell you what.

Spoon a thin layer of ragu over the base of the dish, then add a splatter of bechamel and a sprinkling of mozzarella and Grana Padano. Next, blanch the first round of pasta sheets in the salted boiling water (depending on their size you'll need 2–3 sheets per layer) for 1–2 minutes. Carefully remove the pasta sheets using a spider strainer or two spatulas, then place on a chopping board and trim the corners so they'll fit snugly in your baking dish. Place the pasta in the baking dish, overlapping slightly, then repeat with the remaining ingredients to create three more layers, finishing with a heavy layer of bechamel and grated cheese (make sure you have enough cheese left for this and distribute it evenly, as this will form the crisp topping).

> Here's another real flex move: scatter a dozen cloves of confit garlic through the middle layer of your lasagne, if you like. Oh yeah!

Once your lasagne is assembled, place the baking dish on a large baking tray and cook for 45 minutes, until bubbling and golden brown on top with crispy edges. Rest for a minimum of 15 minutes, then slice and enjoy.

CHICKEN PAELLA WITH PIPIS
JESSE GERNER, BOMBA

Prep time 10–15 minutes
Cook time 1 hour
Serves 8

I love a Sunday long lunch with family and friends, with a couple of glasses of wine and where everyone brings a dish. But I don't want to spend all day in the kitchen, so I've developed this quick, fun and delicious inauthentic paella that still nods to its long history.

If you have a paella pan, that's fantastic, but this can also be done in a frying pan or even a roasting tin. The paella will feed about eight, providing you serve it with a delicious salad and a healthy serving of cheese to snack on.

12 chicken wings

Sea salt and freshly ground black pepper

3 tbsp olive oil

½ **brown onion** finely diced

1 **clove garlic** finely chopped

1 **small red capsicum** finely diced (or use 6 roasted piquillo peppers if you have them)

250ml (1 cup) **passata or diced canned tomatoes**

1 tsp **smoky or sweet paprika** or a combination of both

Pinch of saffron

440g (2 cups) **Bomba or Calasparra rice**

1.5L good-quality chicken stock

400g can **butter beans** or any cooked white beans, rinsed and drained

100g **runner beans or green beans** trimmed, halved if long

200g **pipis** soaked in cold water for 1 hour, drained

2 sprigs rosemary

Lemon wedges to serve

Green salad to serve

Preheat the oven to 190°C.

Cut the chicken wings in half at the joints, then transfer to a roasting tin and season with salt and pepper. Drizzle over 1 tbsp of the olive oil and roast for 25 minutes or until cooked through.

Grab a 35cm paella pan if you have one, or use two large frying pans or a deep roasting tin (just take care not to burn yourself during cooking).

Heat the remaining olive oil in the pan over medium heat, add the onion, garlic and capsicum and cook for 5–6 minutes, until soft. Add the passata or tomatoes, paprika, saffron and rice and stir to combine, then add the stock. Season with salt and pepper, then add the roasted chicken wings, butter beans and green beans. Bring to a simmer and cook, occasionally moving the pan around the flame so it doesn't burn in one spot, for 13 minutes (set a timer).

> I know saffron is expensive, but it really makes the dish; if you want an alternative, Casa Iberica in Fitzroy has a good paella seasoning that's worth checking out.

Push the pipis into the top of the rice and increase the heat to medium–high. Cook for 5 minutes or until the pipis open and the rice has formed a crust on the base (this crisp, caramelised crust is the prized socarrat).

Wave the rosemary over a gas flame for 10–20 seconds, until fragrant, then place it on top of the paella with some lemon wedges.

Enjoy with a glass of white wine or sherry and a simple green salad.

SHORT-RIB TACOS
JULIAN HILLS, NAVI

Prep time 15–20 minutes

Cook time 3 hours, plus
30 minutes resting

Serves 6–8

This is a simple yet delicious way to enhance any Mexican feast. If we're making dinner for friends at home, we find that Mexican is a fun way to eat casually, with great flavours and where guests get to build their meal to their own taste. It's a very relaxed way to eat and is usually accompanied by a couple of beers. We generally serve one or two protein dishes and then a bunch of condiments to "build your own" tacos. It's fun to prepare and there are no rules, as long as you run with the foundation principles of spice, salt and sour. We like to make our own tortillas as well, which is well worth it if you have the time. You can pick up a tortilla press for a few dollars at Casa Iberica in Fitzroy.

2 tsp sea salt

2 tsp freshly ground black pepper

1 tsp cumin seeds

2kg beef short ribs cut into individual ribs (you can ask your butcher to do this for you)

2 tbsp olive oil

2 x 400g cans crushed tomatoes

150g chipotle in adobo sauce

5 cloves garlic

1 brown onion

1 tbsp ground cumin

1 tsp smoked paprika

3 tbsp dried oregano

250ml (1 cup) orange juice

250ml (1 cup) beef stock

2 fresh bay leaves

1 lime halved

Coriander leaves roughly chopped, to serve

Corn tortillas to serve

Capsicum salsa to serve

Diced avocado to serve

Pickled red onion to serve

Preheat the oven to 160°C.

Rub the salt, pepper and cumin seeds into the ribs.

Place a flameproof casserole dish over medium heat and add the olive oil. Working in two batches, sear the ribs for 9–10 minutes, turning frequently to sear all sides and allowing a little of the fat to render to help achieve a nice caramelised flavour.

Meanwhile, place the tomato, chipotle in adobo sauce, garlic, onion, spices and oregano in a blender and blitz until well combined, but not completely smooth.

Set the ribs aside on a plate and drain the excess fat from the dish. Pour the contents of the blender into the dish and cook, stirring, for 3–5 minutes, until the tomatoes start to release their liquid. When you feel the sauce starting to catch (if you start coughing you've gone too far – you're burning the chilli!), pour in the orange juice and bring to the boil. Add the beef stock and bay leaves, then return the ribs to the dish, turning to coat in the sauce (they won't be completely submerged but that's fine).

Now you need to make a cartouche. Cut a piece of baking paper the diameter of your casserole dish. Carefully lay this over the ribs and cover with the lid. Place on the middle shelf of the oven for and cook for 2–2.5 hours.

Remove the lid and cartouche, then turn the ribs over, place the cartouche back on top (but not the lid) and continue to cook for 30 minutes or until the sauce is reduced and the ribs are very tender, but still with some texture and slightly sticky.

Remove the dish from the oven, then rest the ribs in the sauce, covered and turning occasionally, for 30 minutes. Carefully transfer the ribs to a serving dish and spoon over the sauce, then squeeze in the lime juice and scatter with coriander leaves.

To serve, tear the meat from the bone straight into a warmed tortilla and top with capsicum salsa, avocado and pickled onion.

Poultry & Meat

"Chipotle in adobo is smoked dried jalapenos in a paprika tomato sauce. Canned versions are fairly cheap and easy to find these days. I use La Morena. Remove the chipotle seeds, if you want to keep the flavour but reduce the spice."

CHICKEN GIROS SOUVLAKI
KONSTANDAKOPOULOS FAMILY, STALACTITES

Prep time 40–50 minutes, plus overnight straining and 1–2 hours marinating

Cook time about 20 minutes on the grill or about 30 minutes in the oven

Serves 6

Our giros (yeeros, gyros) souvlaki recipe has been in our family for more than 50 years and we have been serving it to Melbournians since 1978. We source all our produce locally and have mostly used the same Melbourne-based suppliers for 43 years.

Adapting this recipe for the home cook and using home appliances has been quite a feat. Kosta, our 94-year-old grandfather, designed and custom-built our rotisseries and skewers to accommodate the size and very large quantities of giros that we cook. Even after 43 years, we still marinate the meat using his original recipe in what we call the traditional Greek way using mati (by the eye), meaning without measurements, and using our experience and knowledge that has been passed down through the generations.

The following recipe is for our chicken giros as it is easier to cook at home; however, the same recipe can be used to make lamb giros – simply substitute the deboned chicken marylands for deboned lamb shoulder. Ask your butcher to cut the lamb for giros. All Greek butchers provide this service.

¼ tsp ground nutmeg

¼ tsp ground cumin

½ tsp hot or smoked paprika

¼ tsp freshly ground black pepper

6 large skinless boneless chicken marylands

3 cloves garlic crushed

1 brown onion finely chopped

2 tsp sea salt

2 tsp sweet paprika

3 tsp dried oregano plus extra if needed

Zest and juice of 1 lemon

70–80g crushed tomatoes blitz fresh tomatoes or use salt-free canned

2 small dollops Greek yoghurt optional

1 tbsp olive oil optional

Home-made chips with salt and dried oregano to serve

→

Start with the tzatziki. Line a fine-meshed sieve with a large square of muslin and add the yoghurt. Set over a bowl and set aside in the fridge overnight to strain. This ensures the tzatziki will be thick and creamy.

The next day, in a small bowl, combine the nutmeg, cumin, hot or smoked paprika and pepper. Place the chicken in a large baking dish in a single layer, then scatter over the garlic, onion, salt, sweet paprika, oregano and the spice mixture. Rub the ingredients onto both sides of the chicken, then add the lemon zest and crushed tomato.

> Good-quality oregano is crucial for this recipe. Look for dried bunches at delicatessens and rub the leaves between your fingertips into small flakes.

Add the yoghurt and olive oil (if using), then mix until the chicken is evenly coated. Cover the chicken and set aside in the fridge to marinate for 1–2 hours.

> We always marinate in this order as this is the way it was passed down from our grandfather, who is a stickler for the exact process being followed in the exact way. Perhaps it's superstition or just tradition, but it always seems to get the best results.

Back to the tzatziki. Cut the cucumber in half lengthways and scrape out the seeds with a spoon. Grate the cucumber, squeeze out the excess liquid, then transfer to a clean tea towel and wring out to remove any remaining liquid.

→

"It's much easier to buy ready-made pita breads. Brands such as Sea Star, Mr Pitta and Gerry's Pittes are all suitable. Alternatively, come to Stalactites and buy a packet."

TZATZIKI

300g thick Greek yoghurt

1 small Lebanese cucumber grated

3 cloves garlic crushed, plus extra

½ tsp white wine vinegar

1 tbsp vegetable oil

Salt flakes and freshly ground
black pepper

PITA BREADS

300g (2 cups) self-raising flour
plus extra for dusting

Large pinch of sea salt

350g Greek yoghurt strained

1 tbsp olive oil

1 tbsp salted butter

SOUVLAKI FILLINGS

1 small brown onion finely sliced

1 tsp finely chopped parsley leaves

2 baby cos or ½ iceberg lettuce
shredded

2–3 tomatoes sliced

Chicken giros souvlaki continued

Place the cucumber in a bowl and add the strained yoghurt, garlic, vinegar and oil and season with salt and pepper. Stir until combined, then taste and add extra garlic or seasoning if required. Cover and set aside in the fridge until ready to serve.

To make the pita breads, sift the flour and salt into a large bowl and add the yoghurt. Mix until you have a large dough ball, then transfer to a lightly floured work surface and knead for 2 minutes until smooth. Divide the dough into six portions, then roll out each portion to a 21–22cm circle, 1–2mm thick.

Heat a little of the oil and butter in a large frying pan over medium–high heat, then add one dough circle and cook for about 1 minute each side until golden and soft. Don't overcook the dough, as the pita breads need to be soft enough to roll. Repeat with the remaining oil, butter and dough to make six pita breads. If using store-bought pita breads, cook in the same way. Keep the warm pitas wrapped in a clean tea towel until ready to serve.

At home giros can be cooked in multiple different ways and still feel as authentic as when cooked on the spit.

To cook the chicken on a barbeque or stovetop, preheat a barbeque or griddle pan over medium–high heat. Add 1 tbsp of olive oil and cook the chicken, in batches if necessary (don't overcrowd the griddle pan or it will drop the temperature too much), for 10 minutes each side or until golden, charred in places and the juices run clear when tested with a skewer. Do not overcook the chicken or it will dry out.

To cook the chicken in an oven, preheat it to 180°C. Place the chicken directly onto a clean oven shelf with a drip tray underneath. Roast for 30–35 minutes, until cooked through.

> If you place a layer of chips in the drip tray as the chicken cooks, they will get the lovely flavour of the chicken as the juices drip onto them.

Once your chicken is cooked, transfer to a plate, squeeze over the lemon juice and season with salt and extra oregano if necessary. Rest for 4 minutes, then cut into strips to resemble giros and keep warm.

Meanwhile, prepare the fillings. Mix the onion and parsley in a bowl and set aside. Grab a friend or family member to help you assemble the souvlakis – you must work quickly as no one wants a cold souvlaki!

Cut six rectangular pieces of baking paper or foil just larger than your pita breads and place on a work surface. Place the bottom half of each pita on the top of half of each rectangle. Spread 1–1½ tbsp of tzatziki onto each pita followed by your chosen amount of chicken, lettuce, tomato and onion and parsley.

Wrap the pitas around the filling. As you roll, lift the end of the paper and wrap it tightly around the souvlaki. Tuck in the end of the paper so the filling doesn't fall out when you pick it up. Continue to roll until your souvlakis are secure.

For an authentic souvlaki experience, serve with home-made chips with salt and dried oregano.

DOUBLE CHEESEBURGER
DANI ZEINI, ROYAL STACKS

Prep time 20 minutes

Cook time about 15 minutes

Serves 4

Until I went to the US for the first time, 100 per cent of my cooking was inspired by European and Middle Eastern cuisines. Up to that point, I had never ordered a burger anywhere other than Maccas, or the occasional "works" burger from my local fish and chip shop. A burger was always a quick hunger fix to me – never a culinary destination, so to speak.

My first burger in the States was at Shake Shack and it blew my mind. It was totally incredible. After that, I ate 30 American burgers on my 34-day trip. I was in love! Discovering these amazing burgers inspired me to begin the Royal Stacks journey back in Melbourne. Since then, burgers have become my life. If I'm going to whip up a burger at home, this recipe is my tried-and-true go-to.

Ingredients make all the difference here. I like Hellmann's mayo for a more traditional sauce, but if you're after more umami, use Japanese Kewpie mayo. If you want a luxurious bun, go for brioche, or look for milk buns if you want something more understated. (The fresher the bun, the better, as it will have a secure exterior and fluffy interior. We need it to absorb fat but still hold the burger together.) I think the best pickles come from those European delis you find in every suburb (you know the ones!), and my preferred cheese is a good-quality sliced cheddar (my favourite comes from Pure Dairy in Doncaster). Look for sliced American burger cheese in any supermarket – something that melts easily and doesn't break apart or burn on the pan. Kraft singles will also do!

1kg good-quality minced beef

Canola oil spray

1 tbsp vegetable oil

16 slices good-quality cheddar

2 tbsp salted butter

4 burger buns such as brioche or milk buns, halved

12 pickle slices

2 large tomatoes cut into 8 even slices

1 large white onion cut into 8 even slices

1 head green oak lettuce leaves separated

→

To make the special sauce, whisk the mayonnaise, ketchup, mustard and spices in a small bowl until well combined. Stir through the chopped gherkin and set aside.

> I like Hellman's mayonnaise and French's Mustard. The ketchup must be Heinz! The others are too sweet. And with paprika, spend a little more on a good one; it makes a huge difference.

Divide the mince into eight 125g balls – the perfect patty size, in my opinion.

> I use a 60/40 blend of pasture-fed brisket and chuck; ask your butcher for this, and to mince it twice: a fine grind and then a coarse grind to achieve the right volume.

Spray a 40cm square of baking paper and a dinner plate with canola oil spray. Working with one meatball at a time, place on the dinner plate and gently press to form burger patties. Be as gentle as possible. If you press too hard they will turn into sausage meat and lose their complexity. You want to retain some air pockets so the fat has a place to escape and sit to give a textural mouthfeel.

→

Poultry & Meat

"Left-over special sauce will keep in an airtight container in the fridge for 5–7 days."

SPECIAL SAUCE

250g (1 cup) whole-egg mayonnaise

2 tbsp tomato ketchup

5 tsp yellow mustard

⅓ tsp garlic powder

¼ tsp smoked paprika

Small pinch of cayenne pepper

80g sweet spiced gherkins chopped

Fries see page 271, to serve

Double cheeseburger continued

Put the pressed patties on the oiled baking paper and set aside. We want to cook them at room temperature to reduce shrinkage.

Heat a touch of vegetable oil (equivalent to a 20-cent coin) in a large non-stick frying pan over high heat. Working in batches, add the patties to the pan and press lightly with a spatula (this will help caramelise the base of the patties), then lightly salt the top of each patty (never salt before placing your patties on the heat!). Cook for 2–2.5 minutes or until you see some moisture on top of the patties, then it's time to flip. Be careful when you do this, as you don't want to break the crust on the other side. To keep them intact, slowly edge your spatula under each patty until it moves freely.

Once flipped, give the patties another gentle press with your spatula, then lay two cheddar slices side by side on top of each patty (don't place them on top of one another) and cook for another 2.5–3 minutes – this will give you a perfectly medium burger. Transfer the burgers to a tray and repeat with the remaining patties. Wipe out the pan and set over medium heat.

Spread the butter over the cut sides of the burger buns, then place, butter side down, in the clean pan and toast for 10–15 seconds until golden brown. Remove from the heat and set aside.

Now it's time to assemble your burgers.

In this order, stack your bottom buns with three pickles, two patties, two tomato slices with a pinch of salt, two onion slices and, finally, the lettuce. I like putting all the fresh ingredients on top so that they aren't steamed by the heat of the patties, and you taste the beef and cheese first. Put a generous teaspoon of special sauce onto the golden side of your top buns and use the back of the spoon to spread it right to the edge – you want every bite to have sauce.

Crown your burger with its top, and enjoy with the fries on page 271.

DORO WAT
DAWIT KEBEDE, MESOB

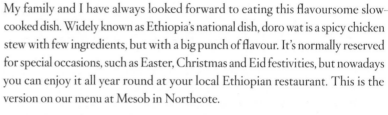

Prep time 30 minutes

Cook time 4 hours

Serves 4–6

My family and I have always looked forward to eating this flavoursome slow-cooked dish. Widely known as Ethiopia's national dish, doro wat is a spicy chicken stew with few ingredients, but with a big punch of flavour. It's normally reserved for special occasions, such as Easter, Christmas and Eid festivities, but nowadays you can enjoy it all year round at your local Ethiopian restaurant. This is the version on our menu at Mesob in Northcote.

Berbere, a spice mix that contains more than 15 ingredients and takes days to prepare, makes this dish what it is. Growing up, I remember my grandmother making berbere for the whole family with the help of my mum, aunts and other relatives and friends. Us kids would play in the front yard, constantly being interrupted by the adults asking us to shoo off the flies and keep the chickens away from the garlic and different varieties of chillies sun-drying on mats. It used to be a challenge for my family and other Ethiopian–Melburnians to find berbere imported from Ethiopia, but now it's readily available at an array of retailers (and at Mesob).

Doro wat is best eaten with injera, a light, fluffy, fermented flatbread that's a staple in Ethiopian cuisine. There are many specialist injera bakeries in the inner-western suburbs of Melbourne. Look for those using flour made from teff (an Ethiopian grain) rather than wheat.

To ease the heat of the dish, we recommend eating doro wat with the condiment ayib, Ethiopia's take on cottage cheese. We've included a quick recipe, which you can make ahead of time and place in the fridge. Otherwise, Greek yoghurt goes nicely as well.

Niter kibbeh (spiced clarified butter) is more difficult. It uses two or three spices that aren't really available in Australia, and there are no good substitutes. You can make niter kibbeh yourself and omit the Ethiopian spices (korarima, besobela and kosseret) or ask your local Ethiopian restaurant for some of their butter.

2kg red onion finely diced

170ml (⅔ cup) neutral-flavoured oil

1 x 1.8kg whole chicken

2 lemons

Sea salt

3 tbsp berbere spice mix add more or less depending on how much spice you like

→

If making ayib, place the yoghurt in a small saucepan set over low heat and stir once. Simmer for 2–3 minutes, until the yoghurt starts to separate, then squeeze in the lemon juice and stir once. Cook for a further 8 minutes or until the yoghurt fully separates and curds start to form. Transfer to a fine-meshed sieve lined with muslin set over a bowl and leave to drain for 10–15 minutes. Place the curds in an airtight container and refrigerate until completely cold and hardened.

→

3 cloves garlic finely chopped

1cm piece of ginger peeled and finely chopped

Pinch of dried korarima (Ethiopian cardamom) or regular ground cardamom

6 hard-boiled eggs

Injera to serve

AYIB

500g (2 cups) plain yoghurt or Greek yoghurt

Juice of 1 lemon

NITER KIBBEH

½ cinnamon quill

½ tsp whole black peppercorns

2 pods korarima (Ethiopian cardamom) or black cardamom

1 tbsp besobela optional

1 tbsp kosseret optional

2 cloves

½ tsp fenugreek seeds

½ tsp coriander seeds

½ tsp oregano

½ tsp cumin seeds

¼ tsp ground nutmeg

¼ tsp ground turmeric

250g butter

¼ brown onion chopped

2 cloves garlic finely chopped

2cm piece ginger finely chopped

Doro wat continued

If making niter kibbeh, toast all the spices in a dry frying pan over low heat for a minute or so, until fragrant. Add the spices to a saucepan with the butter, onion, garlic and ginger and simmer on the lowest heat possible for 1 hour. Be careful not to burn the butter.

Let the mixture cool slightly, then pour through a muslin into a large sterilised jar. This will keep at room temperature for a couple of weeks, and in the fridge for at least a month.

> Doro wat is traditionally cooked with niter kibbeh, but I like to add a dollop just before serving, which is what we do at Mesob.

To make the doro wat, place the onion in a large heavy-based saucepan set over medium heat. Cook (without oil), stirring frequently, for about 40 minutes, until the onion is soft, caramelised and just starting to catch on the base of the pan. Add the oil, reduce the heat to low and continue to cook the onion, stirring frequently, for a further 2 hours or until reduced to a pulpy paste.

Meanwhile, joint the chicken into 12 pieces. Squeeze the juice of one lemon into a large bowl of cold water and add the chicken. Thoroughly wash the chicken in the lemon-infused water, then transfer to a chopping board and remove the skin and any excess fat. Place the chicken in a large clean bowl, then cover with cold water and add 1 tbsp of salt. Slice the remaining lemon and add this to the bowl, then cover with plastic wrap and set aside in the fridge until the onion is ready.

> The cleaning process for the chicken comes from Ethiopia, where most poultry is still slaughtered at home. Even though here in Melbourne we buy our chicken from the butcher, I still always clean the chicken before cooking.

Once the onion has reduced to a paste, stir through the berbere spice mix and continue to cook for a further 30 minutes over low heat until the berbere becomes fragrant. Add 125ml (½ cup) of water and stir well.

Remove the chicken from the fridge and set aside for 10 minutes. Drain and rinse the chicken under cold running water, then add to the pan and gently stir to coat the chicken in the onion and berbere paste. Bring to the boil over medium–low heat, then reduce the heat to low and cook the chicken for 30 minutes. Add 1 tsp of salt, the garlic, ginger and cardamom and stir well, then cover and cook for a further 15 minutes or until the chicken is cooked all the way through.

> You can also make doro wat using boneless chicken thighs; just reduce the cooking time of the chicken to 25 minutes.

Meanwhile, use a fork to gently tear the hard-boiled eggs apart (don't cut all the way through), then add to the pan and gently stir through the sauce.

Pile the doro wat onto injera and place in the middle of the table. Dollop over some niter kibbeh and serve with the ayib on the side for crumbling over.

DJAJ A RIZ (CHICKEN AND RICE)
ABLA AMAD, ABLA'S

Prep time 10–15 minutes
Cook time 1 hour–1 hour 15 minutes
Serves 8

Djaj a riz has become something of a signature dish for me. Generally, it is made for special occasions, but, as I always insist, every meal is a special occasion.

While on a visit to Melbourne more than thirty years ago, an old friend of mine, Barbara, who used to cook for many prominent people in Beirut, showed me the latest trend in presenting the dish in Lebanon. She rummaged through my cupboards for a bowl and instead happened upon a cake tin. In time, I made a slight variation by choosing a tin with a hollow centre, but ever since that day I haven't wavered from creating my chicken and rice dish in a cake tin.

Another way of serving this is to put the lamb and rice mixture on a serving dish and cover it with the chicken. Top with the slivered almonds and pine nuts, and finish with a dusting of ground cinnamon.

---

2 x 500–600g bone-in, skin-on chicken breasts

1 cinnamon quill

2½ tsp sea salt

600g coarsely minced lean lamb

1 tbsp salted butter

½ tsp freshly ground black pepper

½ tsp ground allspice

½ tsp ground cinnamon plus extra to serve

300g (1½ cups) long-grain rice rinsed and drained

2–3 tsp olive oil

70g pine nuts

60g flaked or slivered almonds

Place the chicken breasts in a large saucepan and cover with plenty of cold water. Add the cinnamon quill and 1 tsp of the salt and bring to the boil, then reduce the heat to low and simmer, covered, for 20–30 minutes, until tender and cooked through. Strain, reserving the stock. Remove and discard the skin from the chicken and tear the meat from the bone (the chicken shreds can be any size). Set aside.

Cook the minced lamb in a large saucepan in its own juices over medium heat for 8–10 minutes, mashing with a wooden spoon to break up any lumps and stirring frequently to avoid sticking. Stir in the butter, spices and the remaining salt, then cover and cook, stirring frequently, for 15–20 minutes, until the lamb is well done. Add the rice and 2½ cups (625ml) of the reserved chicken stock, then cover, reduce the heat to medium–low and cook for 15–20 minutes, until the rice is cooked through.

Meanwhile, heat the olive oil in a frying pan over medium heat and cook the pine nuts and almonds, stirring constantly, for 3–4 minutes, until golden. Remove the nuts with a slotted spoon and drain on paper towel.

To assemble, spread the almonds and pine nuts over the base of a round 25cm cake tin with a hollow centre. Pack the shredded chicken around the outer edge of the mould, then fill the mould with the lamb and rice mixture, pressing down firmly with the back of a spoon and ensuring the chicken remains in place.

To serve, place a serving plate over the mould and invert the chicken and rice onto the plate. Gently remove the mould, sprinkle a little extra cinnamon over the top and serve.

"Be adventurous and cook more.
Cookbooks are good, but
you actually have to cook.
There's no way around that."

TADKA
JESSI SINGH, DAUGHTER IN LAW

Prep time 10–15 minutes
Cook time 1 hour
Serves 8

Tadka is two things: a cooking technique, and a spice-infused oil or paste produced using that technique. Known in English as "tempering" or "blooming", tadka involves heating whole or ground spices in hot ghee or another oil to extract their flavour. Without tadka, there would be no curry or Indian food.

When I make tadka at home, I'll always fill four 500ml plastic containers – two litres in total – and put one in the fridge and three in the freezer. In the freezer they'll last for six months. That's the beauty of tadka – it lasts for a long time, then you can quickly cook curries from scratch, rather than buying stuff in jars or packets.

Tadka is the starting point for a whole range of curries from across India, a few of which I've detailed in this recipe. But I encourage you to use your imagination and experiment with whatever meats, seafood and veggies you like.

250ml (1 cup) coconut or mustard oil
20–30 fresh curry leaves to taste
2 tsp cumin seeds or more, to taste
2 tsp mustard seeds or more, to taste
2 large brown onions chopped
2 x 5cm pieces of ginger peeled and chopped
10 cloves garlic chopped
4 large tomatoes diced
2 tbsp garam masala
2 tbsp ground turmeric
2 tbsp ground coriander
2 tbsp ground cumin
8 dried red chillies or more or less, to taste
Sea salt

CHOICE OF PROTEIN
1kg skinless chicken thigh fillets cut into large dice
1kg boneless lamb leg cut into large dice
1kg chuck or blade beef cut into large dice
1kg bone-in goat leg
1kg raw prawns
1kg white fish fillets of your choice
1kg vegetables or legumes

Heat the coconut or mustard oil in a heavy-based frying pan over medium heat. Add the curry leaves, cumin seeds and mustard seeds and cook until they start to crackle and release their aroma, then add the onion and cook, stirring frequently, for 3–5 minutes, until translucent. Add the ginger and garlic and cook for 5 minutes or until you can no longer smell raw garlic, then stir through the tomato, ground spices and chillies and season with salt. Cook for about 5 minutes, adding a little water 1 tbsp at a time to maintain the consistency of a loose paste and to prevent the mixture from sticking to the base of the pan.

> Fresh curry leaves are available at Indian, Sri Lankan, Vietnamese and Thai grocery stores. They're also easy to find at Preston Market, Queen Victoria Market and Prahran Market. A vast majority of the spices sold in Australia come from India, but if you buy at a small specialty grocer you'll get fresher spices that haven't been sitting in a warehouse for a couple of years. I shop at MKS Spices'n Things, an Indian grocer in Preston. There are other branches in Dandenong, Ashburton, Epping and St Albans.

This base can be used to make endless types of curries by simply adding water, milk or coconut milk, along with your choice of protein or vegetables. Use your imagination or follow the ideas below.

To make a Punjabi-style chicken curry, heat half the tadka in a large frying pan over medium heat. Add 1kg of diced chicken thigh fillets and saute for 5 minutes or until browned all over. Add 800ml of water and simmer for a further 5–6 minutes until the chicken is cooked through. Garnish with fresh coriander.
→

Tadka continued

To make a South Indian–style chicken curry, follow the instructions on the previous page to cook the Punjabi-style chicken, then add 800ml of coconut milk and simmer until the chicken is cooked through.

You can replace the chicken with diced lamb leg or beef (ask your local butcher for left-over cuts; cook as per the previous page, then add 800ml of beef stock and simmer for about 1 hour or until tender), young goat (on the bone; cook as per the previous page, then add 800ml of beef stock and simmer for about 1 hour or until tender), raw prawns or white fish fillets (cook as per the previous page, then add 800ml of vegetable stock and simmer for no more than 5 minutes until tender) or your favourite vegetables or legumes, such as potatoes, chickpeas or lentils.

This tadka base can also be used to make tandoori chicken, fish or prawns in an oven or on the barbeque. Simply rub 500g of the tadka, a few salt flakes and the juice of 1 lime into the flesh of four chicken thighs, eight large whole raw prawns or a whole fish fillet (approximately 1kg) of your choice (my favourite is snapper; I use four medium fillets), then cover and set aside in the fridge to marinate for 2–12 hours (the longer you leave it, the better the flavour will be).

Preheat the oven to 200°C, or fire up a barbeque flatplate to medium–hot.

If using chicken thighs, place on a baking tray and cook in the oven for 15 minutes, or on the barbeque for 7 minutes each side until cooked through. Rest, covered, for a few minutes before serving.

If using prawns, place on a baking tray and cook in the oven for 5 minutes, or thread onto skewers and cook on the barbeque for 2–5 minutes, until lightly charred.

If using a whole fish fillet, wrap in foil and cook in a hot oven or on the barbeque for 5 minutes, then remove and leave wrapped in the foil for a further 5 minutes to cook through.

HAINANESE CHICKEN RICE
PHILIP AND SHIRLEY LEONG, GAI WONG

Prep time 40 minutes, plus
4 hours curing

Cook time 2 hours 15 minutes, plus
1 hour cooling and 20 minutes resting

Serves 4

Hainanese chicken rice is a true labour of love. It may seem simple, but there are many elements that must come together to make it complete. As a child, I used to eat this dish at least once a week. Two of my brothers could, in fact, have a whole chicken to themselves, should they have their way. This recipe is also very cost effective for families, as nothing goes to waste and every part of the chicken is used to its fullest potential.

It is important to note that, traditionally, Hainanese chicken rice is eaten cold with hot rice and broth, and with the chilli–garlic sauce on the side. The reason the chicken is served cold is because the important step of cooling the chicken creates the beautiful gelatinous layer between the skin and meat. I usually prepare this dish for dinner as it is a rather long process. Told you, it is a labour of love. If anyone cooks HCR for you, know that you're someone they truly love and care for.

---

1 x 1.5kg whole chicken

Iced water

2 Lebanese cucumbers finely sliced

125ml (½ cup) soy sauce

3 tbsp sesame oil

Sliced spring onion to serve

Coriander sprigs to serve

CHILLI–GARLIC SAUCE

200g long red chillies deseeded if you prefer less spice, roughly chopped

8 cloves garlic

2cm piece of ginger peeled and roughly chopped

130ml freshly squeezed lime juice from about 3 limes

70ml rice wine vinegar

50g raw sugar

2 tsp Himalayan salt

POACHING LIQUID

3 whole chicken carcasses

5 cloves garlic crushed

4–5 makrut lime leaves I like to crush the leaves with my hands first, to release the aromas

→

First up, make the chilli–garlic sauce as it needs to cure for 4 hours. Using a mortar and pestle (or stick blender if you are pushed for time), pound the chilli, garlic and ginger to a fine paste. Transfer to a bowl and stir through the lime juice and vinegar, then add the sugar and salt, stirring slowly until the sugar and salt have dissolved. Set aside for at least 4 hours for the lime and vinegar to work their curing magic. This step is important as it removes the raw taste of the chilli, garlic and ginger.

Before making the poaching liquid, it's important to thoroughly clean the chicken carcasses. According to our elders, this process removes the dirt and scum from the bones, thus giving you a beautiful clear broth at the end. To do this, place the carcasses in a large (10L) stockpot and cover with water. Bring to the boil over high heat and blanch for about 10 minutes or until most of the scum rises to the top. Drain and wash the carcasses under cool running water to remove any last vestiges of scum on the bones. Clean and wipe dry the stockpot.

Next, place 8L of water in your now clean stockpot and bring to the boil. Add the chicken carcasses and the remaining poaching liquid ingredients, then reduce to a simmer and cook for 1.5 hours or until the chicken carcasses are soft to touch. To test the carcasses, gently squeeze the bones with a pair of tongs (don't worry if they come apart, this is perfectly fine). This releases additional flavour from the chicken bones into the stock.

Loosely tie the whole chicken to a long cooking chopstick or wooden spoon, one that will sit comfortably across the top of the pot. To do this, loop a length of string under the wings and then attach it to the chopstick or spoon.

→

Poultry & Meat

2cm piece of ginger unpeeled

1 tsp whole white peppercorns

1 tsp Himalayan salt

FRAGRANT RICE

500g jasmine rice

750ml (3 cups) poaching liquid

2 pandan leaves tied in a knot

3cm piece of ginger peeled and smashed using the side of a knife

½ tsp Himalayan salt

Hainanese chicken rice continued

This enables the chicken to hang suspended in the poaching liquid, rather than sitting on the base of the pot, allowing the chicken to remain intact and visually silky.

Using tongs, remove the chicken carcasses from the poaching liquid and discard. Bring the liquid back to the boil, then, holding onto the chopstick or spoon, gently dunk the chicken in and out of the liquid three to four times. This process is important as it tightens the chicken skin. (Many recipes will tell you to stuff aromatics into the cavity of the chicken. Please don't do this, as it will actually stop the beautiful poaching liquid from entering the cavity of the chicken.)

Quickly reduce the heat to a gentle simmer, then slowly lower the chicken into the pot, with the chopstick or spoon resting on top. The chicken must be completely submerged in the poaching liquid without touching the base or side of the pot; otherwise the skin will be damaged. Top up with extra boiling water, if necessary.

Simmer for 30 minutes, then remove the pot from the heat. Cover with foil and allow the chicken to continue poaching in the liquid for another 10 minutes.

Meanwhile, fill a bowl large enough to submerge the chicken with iced water. This is a vital process as it stops the cooking process. It also ensures you'll have a silky gelatinous layer between the skin and the meat. Remove the chicken from the poaching liquid (reserve the poaching liquid) and submerge it in the iced water. Set aside for 1 hour, then remove the chicken and allow to air dry for 20 minutes.

To make the fragrant rice, wash the rice two or three times in cold water, until the water runs clear. Drain, then transfer to a rice cooker or saucepan and add the remaining rice ingredients, ensuring that the pandan leaves and ginger are on top of the rice. Cook according to the rice cooker instructions or simmer in the pan for 10 minutes or until the liquid is absorbed. Remove from the heat, cover and set aside for 10 minutes, until fluffy and cooked through.

Taste the remaining reserved poaching liquid and add salt and white pepper, to taste.

To serve, cut the chicken into bite-sized pieces. At home, we usually serve it on the bone, but you can also debone the chicken if you prefer. Lay the cucumber slices on four plates and top with the chicken, then drizzle over the soy sauce and sesame oil. Divide the broth among small serving bowls. Add spring onion and coriander to each dish, to taste. Place the rice and chilli–garlic sauce on the table and invite everyone to sit down. Address your elders at the table by saying: chiak peng! (Let's eat!).

To eat, we usually douse our fragrant rice with the soy sauce and sesame oil from the chicken and mix it thoroughly. Then, to achieve the perfect bite, we pile a little rice, chicken and chilli–garlic sauce onto a spoon and eat it in one gulp. Only after a few bites do we go in for the cucumber at that bottom of the plate, after it has absorbed the beautiful sauce. The cucumber provides a wonderful fresh taste, almost like a palate cleanser, between bites of rice and chicken. This is why we can eat this dish every single day and never get bored.

Poultry & Meat

Minh Phat, Abbotsford

AYAM PERCIK (BARBEQUED CHICKEN)
TONY TAN, TONY TAN COOKING SCHOOL

Prep time 25–30 minutes, plus overnight marinating

Cook time about 50 minutes, plus 10 minutes resting

Serves 4–6

This incredibly fragrant grilled ayam (chicken) comes from the Malaysian state of Kelantan, on the northeast coast of the peninsula. It's commonly found at night markets and roadside stalls, cooking over coconut embers. But the dish's extreme popularity has sent it all over the country, even reaching Kuala Lumpur's high-end restaurants.

The original lemongrass and coconut milk marinade is sweet and relatively mild. Nowadays, many chefs – myself included – prefer this version, the spicier ayam percik utara (utara means "north"), which includes cardamom, cloves and chillies. But it's quite flexible, and you can adjust the spicy, sweet, earthy and sour flavours to suit your taste. The sauce is thickened using candlenuts and its sweetness is balanced by dried asam gelugor, a sour fruit native to Malaysia. If you can't find it, use lemon peel or tamarind pulp instead.

For me, this chicken is pure summer. It's the first thing I think of when I feel like barbecuing. I like to eat it with a refreshing tomato, cucumber and chopped coriander salad, finished with a squeeze of lime. Grab a beer or a crisp white wine and enjoy.

---

1 x 1.8kg whole chicken

3 tbsp vegetable oil

2 lemongrass stalks white part only, bashed using the side of a knife

2 pieces asam gelugor

2 makrut lime leaves

2 cloves

3 cardamom pods

1 tbsp caster sugar

400ml can coconut milk

Sea salt

Rice and salad to serve

CHICKEN MARINADE

1–2 tsp chilli powder

2 tsp ground turmeric

1 tsp sugar

Good pinch of sea salt

→

To butterfly the chicken, lay it on a chopping board breast side down. With a pair of poultry shears or kitchen scissors, cut along both sides of the backbone and remove it, then press down on the breastbone to flatten the bird. Working from the neck, cut through the cartilage that connects the breastbone to the ribs, then run your fingers along the sides of the breastbone and tease it out. Trim off any fat and discard, then wipe the chicken dry and make a few slashes on the thickest parts of the legs and breasts.

Combine the chicken marinade ingredients in a bowl, then sprinkle over the chicken and pop it in a zip-lock bag and seal. Massage well and set aside in the fridge to marinate overnight.

To make the spice paste, drain the dried chillies and reserve the soaking water. Roughly chop the chillies. Working in batches, pound the chillies and the remaining spice paste ingredients using a mortar and pestle to a medium paste, adding a little of the reserved chilli soaking water if necessary to get things going.

Heat the vegetable oil in a large frying pan over medium–high heat, add the spice paste, lemongrass, asam gelugor, lime leaves, cloves and cardamom pods and saute for 5–6 minutes, until fragrant. Add the sugar, coconut milk and 250ml (1 cup) of water, then reduce the heat to medium and simmer, stirring occasionally, for 7–10 minutes, until the sauce thickens slightly.

→

218

Prahran Market, South Yarra

SPICE PASTE

8–10 dried red chillies soaked in hot water for 20–30 minutes

5 golden shallots roughly chopped

4 candlenuts

3cm piece of ginger peeled and roughly chopped

3cm piece of galangal peeled and roughly chopped

3 cloves garlic peeled

1 lemongrass stalk white part only, finely sliced

Ayam percik (barbequed chicken) continued

Season with salt to taste and discard the lemongrass and lime leaves. Remove the pan from the heat and set aside one-third of the sauce to serve with the chicken.

Allow the chicken to come to room temperature.

Meanwhile, prepare a charcoal barbeque. When the glowing coals have a light coating of ash, place the chicken, skin side down, on the grill and cook, turning occasionally and basting it now and then with the remaining coconut sauce for 35–40 minutes, until nicely charred and the juices run clear when the thickest part of the chicken is tested with a skewer.

> In Malaysia, most cooks use coconut charcoal. I prefer binchotan, the Japanese white charcoal. You can also use a gas grill or oven, but the chicken won't taste quite the same. I like to char over medium–low heat so the chicken remains moist and still forms a crust from the constant basting.

Rest the chicken for 10 minutes, then cut into portions and serve with the reserved coconut sauce, rice and salad.

Poultry & Meat

ROAST CHICKEN
PHILIPPE MOUCHEL, PHILIPPE

Prep time 15 minutes,
plus overnight marinating

Cook time 1 hour 10 minutes,
plus 20 minutes resting

Serves 4

1 x 1.5kg whole chicken
with neck still attached

Olive oil for rubbing

Sea salt and ground white pepper

1 bouquet garni using thyme, bay
leaves and rosemary

1 Moroccan preserved lemon
quartered (or use fresh lemon)

400ml chicken stock or water

Few drops of white wine vinegar

HERB BUTTER

100g soft salted butter plus extra
for brushing

1 tbsp Dijon mustard

Handful of mixed herbs such as
parsley, tarragon, sage, coriander
and chervil, roughly chopped

5 cloves garlic finely chopped

Sea salt and ground white pepper

At home in Normandy, where I grew up with my brothers and sisters (we were a big family), we had this huge garden with all kinds of vegetables. We also had chickens and rabbits and ducks, so every Sunday my father used to kill either a chicken or a duck for the family lunch. This recipe reminds me of my father and those Sunday lunches.

We would put the bird in the oven, go to church and when we got back everything was ready to eat. The vegetables would change depending on what was growing in the garden. In winter, we'd have carrots and potatoes; in spring, cabbage and leeks. In summer, a simple tomato salad with a vinaigrette was hard to beat.

Cooking isn't always about a recipe, it's about going to the market and seeing what's there. I still go to the market every Sunday – either Queen Victoria Market or South Melbourne Market. Those markets are especially good for finding quality chicken. For French ingredients, I like to go to The Essential Ingredient in South Melbourne.

When I first started working at Paul Bocuse, it was winter so the fireplace in the dining room was going all the time – it smelled beautiful. We used to cook chicken and duck and squab in that fire and I was in charge. It was fantastic. Since then, I've always had roast chicken on my menu.

To make the herb butter, combine the ingredients in a small bowl with a spoon, then transfer to a piping bag and set aside (do not refrigerate).

Preheat the oven to 220°C (fan-forced).

Using a sharp knife, remove the neck from chicken, then chop it into small pieces and set aside.

> It's important to put the left-over neck pieces and anything else you don't use in the roasting tin. It will help with making the jus.

Loosen the chicken skin by delicately sliding oiled fingers under the breast and legs to detach it from the flesh. Make sure not to break the skin.

Snip about 3cm from the end of the piping bag. On one side of the chicken, gently place the piping bag under the skin, pushing it down one side towards the leg, then squeeze and release half the herb butter. Repeat on the other side, then use your hands to evenly spread the butter underneath the chicken skin. Season the cavity with salt and white pepper and add the bouquet garni and lemon.

→

Roast chicken continued

Next, truss the chicken with kitchen string. This process is very important as it helps the chicken to cook evenly. I trussed hundreds of chicken while working for Paul Bocuse in France.

There, we used a trussing needle and he was very particular about the way it had to be done. Don't worry, for home cooking a needle is unnecessary and trussing can be easily done by hand. Simply slide a 50cm length of kitchen string under the chicken's ribcage and tie the breast, catching the wings, in a tight knot. With another 50cm length of kitchen string, tie the legs together.

Take your chicken out of the fridge an hour before you roast it, so it comes to room temperature. It will cook better this way.

Generously brush the chicken with extra soft butter, but do not season with salt, as this will soften the skin.

Place the chicken, breast side up, in a roasting tin that will fit it snugly and add the chopped neck. (If the tin is too large the extra fat from the chicken will burn and smoke.) Roast the chicken for about 15 minutes, until the skin starts to colour, then reduce the temperature to 180°C and roast for another 30 minutes, rotating the roasting tin once or twice to obtain an even cooking and colour.

To test if the chicken is cooked, insert a kitchen thermometer into the thickest part of a leg – the temperature should be 70–72°C. If you don't have a kitchen thermometer, use a skewer and prick the leg between the joint. If the juice runs clear, the chicken is cooked. Remove from the oven, cover loosely with foil and rest for 20 minutes.

Remove the legs from the chicken and cut into two at the joint, then remove the breasts and carve into two as well. Keep warm.

Cut the carcass into pieces and saute with the fat in the roasting tin over medium–high heat for 2 minutes. Add 100ml of the chicken stock or water and cook until evaporated, then add another 100ml of the stock or water and repeat the process. Add the remaining stock or water and reduce by half. Pass this natural chicken jus through a fine-meshed sieve into a jug and stir through a few drops of white wine vinegar.

Arrange the chicken on a serving plate and serve with the jus on the side and your choice of accompaniments – I like sauteed potatoes or seasonal vegetables.

Meatsmith, Fitzroy

"Shop for good
ingredients. When you
start with a bad product,
meat especially, it's very
hard to fix that with
any kind of advice."

DUCK CURRY
ADAM D'SYLVA, CODA

Prep time 10–15 minutes,
plus overnight marinating
Cook time 60–75 minutes
Serves 8

I love the richness and gaminess of duck. It has a reputation for being luxurious and hard to cook, but it's not really. The method here is what we used when I was head chef at Pearl, Geoff Lindsay's restaurant in Richmond. Geoff and Martin Boetz, who I worked with at Longrain, have been two of my biggest influences.

Similar to Peking duck, the skin is marinated in sugar, which helps it caramelise nicely in the oven. And the roasting tin is filled with coconut milk and whatever aromatic scraps you have on hand, such as makrut lime leaves, ginger, lemongrass and Thai basil. It's a bit like a bouquet garni.

Once the duck is cooked, this coconut milk can be reused in the curry itself. The flavour from the duck and the aromatics really take it to the next level.

This is my favourite curry sauce to make and eat, and it's been on the menu at Coda since we opened in 2009. People still rate it, and I have to cook it everywhere I go; otherwise they ask, "Where's your duck curry? Where's your duck curry? Where's your duck curry?"

375ml (1½ cups) soy sauce I like Healthy Boy brand

1 tsp white peppercorns crushed

3 tbsp caster sugar plus extra if needed

4 duck marylands

2 x 400ml cans coconut milk

1 red banana chilli

3 makrut lime leaves

1 lemongrass stalk white part only, bruised and roughly chopped

270ml coconut cream

100g palm sugar shaved

100ml fish sauce

200ml chicken stock

YELLOW CURRY PASTE

1 red onion chopped

8 cloves garlic

6 coriander roots scraped and cleaned

4cm piece of turmeric peeled and chopped

→

Place the soy sauce, crushed white peppercorns and sugar in a non-reactive (glass, ceramic or stainless steel) container, then whisk to dissolve the sugar. Taste the marinade – it should taste more sweet than salty, so add more sugar if needed. Add the duck, skin side down, then seal with a lid and leave to marinate in the fridge overnight.

> I've been buying my duck at Kevin's Poultry at Prahran Market for 20 years.

The next day, preheat the oven to 150°C.

Place the duck in a snug-fitting roasting tin, skin side up. Pour in one of the cans of coconut milk, along with the banana chilli, lime leaves and lemongrass. Roast for 1.5 hours.

Meanwhile, to make the curry paste, place the onion, garlic, coriander roots, turmeric and ginger in a heavy-based saucepan or wok over medium heat. Add 2 tbsp of water and cook, stirring, for 5–6 minutes, until the ingredients are lightly coloured and soft. Add a little more water if they start to burn – you want the ingredients to caramelise, which will give the finished curry depth and added flavour.

→

MINH PHAT

"Pickled krachai
is similar to pickled
ginger; I buy it from
Minh Phat off Victoria
Street, Abbotsford."

Minh Phat, Abbotsford

4cm piece of ginger peeled and chopped

8 dried long red chillies deseeded and soaked in hot water for 20–30 minutes, drained

SPICE MIX

1 tbsp coriander seeds

1 tsp cumin seeds

1 tsp fennel seeds

½ tsp white peppercorns

2 tbsp sea salt

TO SERVE

Coriander leaves

Pickled krachai

Crispy fried shallots

Steamed white rice

Duck curry continued

Transfer the mixture to a large bowl and add the drained chillies. Set aside to cool, then blitz in a food processor for 3–4 minutes to a smooth, reddish-yellow paste.

If the paste is not wet enough, add a little water to help move the blades.

To make the spice mix, wet the coriander seeds, then toast over medium heat in a small heavy-based frying pan or wok, for 2–3 minutes, until fragrant and lightly coloured. Set aside. Repeat with the cumin seeds, followed by the fennel seeds. Using a mortar and pestle, grind the toasted seeds and white peppercorns to a fine powder, then stir through the curry paste along with the salt until combined.

To make the curry, place a heavy-based saucepan over medium heat. Add the coconut cream, bring to the boil and cook for 8–10 minutes, until the cream splits. Add 100g of the curry paste and fry for 2–3 minutes, until fragrant and you can smell the spices. Add the palm sugar and fish sauce and cook, stirring, until the sugar is dissolved. Pour in the remaining can of coconut milk and the stock, bring to the boil, then reduce the heat to a simmer and cook for 20–25 minutes, until reduced slightly.

Divide the sauce among four shallow bowls and add the duck. Garnish with coriander leaves, pickled krachai and crispy fried shallots and serve with white rice on the side.

Left-over curry paste will keep in an airtight container in the fridge for up to 2 weeks.

WHOLE ROAST DUCK WITH ORANGE
BRIGITTE HAFNER, TEDESCA OSTERIA

Prep time 10 minutes

Cook time about 2 hours 30 minutes, plus 25 minutes resting

Serves 4

1 whole duck

1 **carrot** roughly chopped

2 **celery stalks** roughly chopped

1 **large brown onion** roughly chopped

1 **orange** stabbed several times with a sharp knife

2 **dried bay leaves**

250ml (1 cup) **red wine**

1½–2 tsp **salt flakes**

QUATRE ÉPICES

1 tsp **black peppercorns**

6 **cloves**

1 **whole nutmeg**

1 **cinnamon quill**

Roast duck is one of my all-time favourite dishes. Cooking duck is not as hard as you might think because it is quite a forgiving meat, with a good amount of fat to help keep it moist. My number-one rule is to buy a genuine free-range duck as they just have so much more flavour and a better texture. I buy duck from a specialist poultry supplier and it's definitely worth the extra cost and effort.

When you roast a whole duck, you get more flavour from cooking the meat on the bone as well as retaining moisture. I like to cook it all the way through so the meat is well done – for me, this is the most delicious way to eat it, plus it's easier to carve. You also get quite a bit of duck fat, which you can save to make the best roast potatoes.

If this is for a dinner party, I often roast the duck in the afternoon and then simply reheat it for 15 minutes in a hot oven before carving it at the table. Alternatively, wait for the duck to cool a little after roasting, then carve off the legs and breasts before later reheating. Serve with a good-quality bottle of wine for any special occasion.

Preheat the oven to 175°C. Rinse the duck and pat dry with paper towel.

Place the carrot, celery and onion in a roasting tin and sit the duck on top. Stuff the duck cavity with the orange and bay leaves, then pour over the wine.

To make the quatre épices, use a spice grinder to grind the spices to a fine powder, then sprinkle generously over the duck and season with the salt.

Transfer to the oven and roast for 1.5–2 hours (depending on the size of the duck), until the juices run clear when the thickest part of the thigh is pierced with a skewer. Carefully pour the juices from the tin into a glass measuring jug, while you rest the duck, covered, for 25 minutes. Discard the vegetables.

> It's super important to rest the meat for at least 20 minutes, as this ensures the flavours come together really well, and the texture of the meat is superior. The combination of the orange, red wine and mirepoix results in a delicious sauce that really helps to make the dish sing.

To make the sauce, let the fat settle on the top of the jug, then remove using a ladle or a spoon (the fat can be kept in an airtight container in the freezer for up to 3 months). Pull out the orange from the duck cavity, and when cool enough to handle squeeze it into the sauce. Pour the sauce into a small saucepan, then reduce over medium–high heat for 3–4 minutes. Pour into a serving jug and serve with the duck.

"I highly recommend buying your duck from The Chicken Pantry at Queen Vic Market."

CIDER-BRINED PORK CHOPS
ALMAY JORDAAN, OLD PALM LIQUOR

Prep time 10 minutes, plus overnight brining

Cook time 20–25 minutes, plus 10 minutes resting

Serves 4

At home I mostly cook on a braai – a South African barbeque. In the lead up to opening Old Palm Liquor with my partner, Simon Denman, we'd spend the day at the site, then come home and test something for dinner.

These pork chops took about six months to develop and appeared on our first menu. In testing I found there were a few things that had to be just right for the recipe to really succeed. The length of time the pork spent in the brine was really important, as was the temperature of the fire. And the addition of oyster sauce to the marinade made a big difference.

The pork doesn't need to be served with a sauce: the marinade already does so much to preserve its juiciness. Instead, I like it paired with a fresh salad of peas and pickled shallots. If you use fresh young peas, you get a unique sweetness that goes really well with the pork. And the tangy pickled shallots and fresh mint are really complementary, too.

---

4 x 250 g bone-in pork loin chops with 2cm fat attached

2½ tbsp grapeseed oil

2½ tbsp oyster sauce

Salt flakes and freshly ground black pepper

Juice of ½ lemon

BRINE

1.9L apple cider

125g (½ cup) sea salt not iodised table salt!

100g soft brown sugar

80g young ginger smashed using a mortar and pestle

1 lemon cut into 1cm thick slices

2 dried bay leaves torn

5 black peppercorns crushed

Pea salad with pickled shallots see page 268, to serve

For this recipe, I like to use a raised grill over mallee root charcoal, but you can use any charcoal you have on hand, or a regular gas barbeque.

Start by brining the pork chops the day before you want to cook. Gently heat half the cider in a saucepan over medium heat, then add the salt and sugar and stir until dissolved. Transfer to a non-reactive (glass, ceramic or stainless steel) container large enough to hold the pork chops and add the ginger, lemon, bay leaves and peppercorns. Stir through the remaining cold cider to cool the mixture down, then chill in the fridge until completely cold. Add the pork chops, making sure they are completely submerged in the liquid, then leave in the fridge overnight.

> Buy the best pork you can find from a reputable butcher, such as Mathews Artisan Butchers, Meatsmith, Cannings or Hagen's Organics.

At least 2 hours before you want to serve the pork chops, light a charcoal barbeque, with a clean grill sitting at least 20cm above the coals. While the embers are burning down, make a marinade by combining the grapeseed oil and oyster sauce in a shallow dish. Add the pork chops and turn to coat in the marinade, then set aside for 1 hour at room temperature.

> Oyster sauce contains added MSG, which I don't have a problem with for this recipe. It's just a tiny bit and really boosts the umami flavour of the meat. There's also a bit of caramel in there, giving the meat a lovely crusty surface that's hard to achieve otherwise. I use oyster sauce on steak as well, although not the big premium cuts. It's similar to how some chefs brush their meat with koji.

→

Cider-brined pork chops continued

Your fire is ready when the flames have died down and you can just hover your hand 30cm above the coals for 3–4 seconds – the heat should not be too fierce; otherwise it will be impossible to control the pork fat dripping onto the coals and creating flames.

If using a gas barbeque, preheat it to high for 20 minutes – you should be able to hold your hand 30cm above the grill for 3–4 seconds.

Season the chops with salt and pepper and lay them on the grill, keeping a close eye for flames (you might need to move the chops around a bit). Turn the chops over every few minutes, to ensure the caramel in the oyster sauce doesn't cause them to darken and burn before they are cooked through – don't walk away at this stage of the cooking process!

Continue to cook the pork chops for 20 minutes or until the thickest part of the meat reaches an internal temperature of 56–57°C when tested with a kitchen thermometer. For the last 5 minutes of cooking, turn the chops with the fat towards the coals and balance them up against each other in an A-frame shape (this will render the remaining fat a little – continue to watch for flame flare-ups).

Squeeze over the lemon juice, then remove the pork chops from the grill and rest on a wire rack, covered, for 10 minutes.

Divide the pork chops among plates and serve with my pea salad with pickled shallots on page 268.

OSSO BUCO
MARCO FINANZIO, UMBERTO ESPRESSO BAR

Prep time 20 minutes
Cook time about 4 hours
Serves 4

Osso buco is a specialty of the Lombardy region in Italy's north. It is traditionally served with risotto or polenta depending on where in the region it is served. Some of my strongest food memories from my travels to Italy over the years are of cold winter nights spent in trattorie di Lombardia, enjoying osso buco with polenta and a nice glass of full-bodied Barolo.

Osso buco is a cross-cut of veal shank and literally translates to "bone hole". Traditionally, the cut was inexpensive, but there is no such thing these days. Go to a butcher you trust and ensure your cow lived a happy life. We always buy free range and grass fed.

This recipe is a slight riff on the classic, but you can also make it with white wine – known as osso buco in bianco – cinnamon and bay leaves, and serve it with gremolata. The marrow gives this dish that unmistakable kick in the culo, making it one of our favourite staples. Osso buco never wants to leave our menu, but it would be wrong to have it on all year round. Bring on winter and bring on the braises.

125ml (½ cup) extra-virgin olive oil
4 veal osso buco
50g plain flour for dusting
50g prosciutto cut into 2 cm dice
300g button mushrooms finely sliced
40g carrot finely diced
45g red capsicum finely diced
1 tbsp tomato paste
750ml bottle good-quality red wine
1 sprig rosemary
4 sprigs thyme
5 fresh or dried bay leaves
1 tbsp black peppercorns
750ml (3 cups) vegetable stock
1½ tbsp salted butter
Salt flakes and freshly ground black pepper
Polenta to serve

All the work here is done in the prep. The method is quite straightforward and it's a classic one-pot wonder for home. Be sure to have all your ingredients prepped and measured before you start, as this will reduce unnecessary stress during the cooking process and you can confidently start making some headway into a good bottle of vino.

Preheat the oven to 180°C.

Place a flameproof casserole dish over medium heat and add the olive oil. Wait a couple of minutes for the oil to get smoking hot, then quickly dust the osso buco in the flour, add them to the dish and sear for about 2 minutes each side, until browned. This will lock in the juices and help keep the meat tender while cooking.

> If you find that the osso buco start to curl up at the sides, use a sharp knife to carefully nick the outer fat. This will relax the osso buco and leave you with a more pleasing flat shape. This is a good little trick that is not often taught and will allow for more even cooking.

Once the osso buco are seared, remove from the dish and set aside.

Whatever you do, leave all the good stuff in the bottom of the dish, as this will be the base for the rich sauce. Add the prosciutto to the dish and saute over medium–low heat until golden brown and all the fat has rendered. Add the mushroom, carrot and capsicum and cook for 1–2 minutes, until the vegetables have softened, then add the tomato paste and cook for another minute.

→

Poultry & Meat

Osso buco continued

Deglaze the dish with 100ml of the red wine and give everything a good stir. This will dissolve all the goodness stuck to the bottom of the dish.

Return the seared osso buco to the dish, throw in the rosemary, thyme, bay leaves and peppercorns, then pour in the remaining red wine and the vegetable stock. There's no need to add any seasonings at this stage; save this until the end.

Cut a piece of baking paper the same size as your dish and carefully place this over the osso buco. Pop the lid on, then transfer to the oven and cook for 3 hours. At this stage, the meat should almost start to fall off the bone when tested with a fork. If it's not (you'll know), keep going for another solid 30 minutes and check again. By this time, the aromas in your kitchen will definitely have the neighbours interested.

Once the meat is ready, if the sauce is not thick enough (it should easily coat the back of a spoon), carefully remove the osso buco, then return the dish to the stovetop and cook, stirring to prevent the sauce sticking to the base of the dish, over low heat until reduced slightly. For added richness, add the butter, then taste and season with salt and pepper if necessary.

Serve with fresh, soft polenta (instant is absolutely fine, simply follow the packet instructions as some vary). At Umberto Espresso Bar, we deep-fry the polenta to give it texture. Divide the polenta among plates, top with the osso buco and evenly pour the rich, salty sauce over the top.

I promise this dish will be a hit and will feature as regularly on your menu as it does on ours.

Prahran Market, South Yarra

BOEUF BOURGUIGNON
GERAUD FABRE, FRANCE-SOIR

Prep time 30–35 minutes

Cook time 3 hours

Serves 8

I started at France-Soir in 1995 and took over as head chef in 2000, but this boeuf bourguignon has been on the menu since the restaurant opened in 1986. It's a consistent seller. People like it because it's hearty, warm and homely. It's just good comfort food. And there's nothing complicated about cooking it at home, as long as you're not afraid of the clean-up afterwards.

Every region in France has their own version of boeuf bourguignon. Where I'm from, near Bordeaux, we use the same cut of beef and similar vegetables, but instead of using a Burgundy wine, we use one from Bordeaux. The ingredients may change depending on what part of France you're in, but the basic techniques and method will always be the same: sear some meat, season it, add vegetables, cover in wine, stock, mustard – whatever – and slow-cook it. You will always end up with something tasty.

The better quality ingredients you use, the better your dish will taste. And that's also true for wine. Reducing the wine concentrates the flavour, but it also takes away a wine's subtleties – and subtlety is the difference between a good wine and a great wine. So cask wine will taste fine here, but if you have access to a good-quality wine, then I encourage you to use that. Just don't waste a 1934 Chateau Margaux on this boeuf bourguignon!

1.5L red wine

150ml duck fat or vegetable oil

1.5kg oyster blade steak ask your butcher to dice it into 70g chunks

Sea salt

200g kaiserfleisch diced

1 large brown onion diced

1 celery stalk finely diced

¼ red capsicum finely diced

25g plain flour sifted

2L veal or vegetable stock

1 bouquet garni using thyme, bay leaves, parsley stalks and leek tops

1 tsp tomato paste

2 carrots cut into 16 pieces

500g button mushrooms quartered

Freshly ground black pepper

Roast or mashed potatoes to serve

Pour the wine into a saucepan set over medium heat and simmer for 1 hour or until it reduces to a third of its original volume. Keep warm.

Meanwhile, heat one-third of the fat or oil in a large flameproof casserole dish over medium–high heat. Season the steak with 2–3 tsp of salt, then, working in small batches, sear the steak on all sides until browned. This will take about 20 minutes – try not to rush this process by overcrowding the dish. Set aside on a plate and discard the fat or oil.

> Duck fat has a high smoke point and adds another flavour dimension to the dish, but I realise not everyone has duck fat at home, so vegetable oil works, too. But if you've got duck fat, it makes everything better.

Wipe the dish clean, then place over medium–high heat again and add the remaining fat or oil. Add the kaiserfleisch, onion, celery and capsicum and saute for about 8 minutes, until the onion is translucent.

Return the steak and its juices to the dish and stir to combine, then add the flour and stir until the ingredients are well coated.

→

France-Soir, South Yarra

Boeuf bourguignon continued

Add the reduced wine and stock, ensuring that the steak and vegetables are completely submerged, then add the bouquet garni and bring to the boil. Reduce the heat to a rapid simmer and cook for 30 minutes. Add the tomato paste, carrot and mushroom, then reduce the heat to a gentle simmer and continue to cook, covered, for 2 hours or until the meat is completely tender and soft to touch.

Season with salt and pepper, to taste.

Discard the bouquet garni and let the bourguignon rest, covered, for about 30 minutes. The flavour will improve with time, and it will taste even better the next day.

Serve with roast or mashed potatoes.

BISTECCA ALLA FIORENTINA
ANDREAS PAPADAKIS, OSTERIA ILARIA

Prep time 5 minutes

Cook time about 30 minutes

Serves 3–4

This is a party-sized steak and I cook it whenever I have a couple of friends over for dinner. Traditionally, this Florentine steak is made only from Chianina beef, one of the oldest – and largest – cattle breeds in the world. While it's hard to find in Australia, there is a small farm in South Gippsland called Isola Chianina that raises grass-fed animals. But really, any good-quality grass-fed steak will do.

The salsa verde is an easy and really delicious recipe that I use as a condiment for most proteins cooked on the barbeque. It works very well with sardines, calamari, ox tongue, sausage and, of course, any type of steak. The quality of the ingredients is crucial, though. Make sure you get your parsley from your local grocer or market rather than the supermarket. I like to use brined Lilliput capers and Italian or Spanish anchovy fillets in olive oil.

---

1 x 750g–1kg T-bone steak
at least 5cm thick

Sea salt and freshly ground
black pepper

1 sprig rosemary or sage
leaves picked

SALSA VERDE

½ bunch parsley leaves picked
and chopped

3 anchovy fillets

30g capers rinsed and drained

1 small clove garlic

125ml (½ cup) olive oil

25ml sherry vinegar

Charred broccolini, macadamia
and capers see page 271, to serve

Remove the steak from the fridge at least 2 hours before you want to cook. Season really well with salt and pepper and rub with the herbs.

To make the salsa verde, place the ingredients in a measuring jug, then blitz using a stick blender until smooth. Set aside.

Preheat a barbeque grill plate to medium.

Place the steak upright on the barbeque, fat side down, and cook for 10 minutes. A good trick is to put a pair of metal tongs around it, so the steak doesn't fall on its side. I find this caramelises the fat really well and also tempers the meat without overcooking it.

Increase the heat to the highest setting and flip the steak, so it's meat side down on the barbeque. Cook for 5–6 minutes each side for rare, 7–8 minutes each side for medium-rare or 9–10 minutes each side for medium. The steak is meant to be rare to medium-rare, but it is always better to undercook your steak than overcook it. Let it rest on a wire rack for 10 minutes while you cook the broccolini.

When you are ready to serve, return the steak to the barbeque for 30 seconds each side to warm through, checking the internal temperature reaches 52°C for rare, 55°C for medium-rare or 60°C for medium on a kitchen thermometer. It is tricky to master a barbeque grill so using a meat thermometer is the most accurate way to ensure the meat is cooked to your liking.

For a large steak like this one, I always remove the bone and carve into thick slices before I put it on the table. Serve with the salsa verde and my charred broccolini, macadamia and capers on page 271.

Poultry & Meat

ROAST LAMB SHOULDER
SCOTT PICKETT, ESTELLE

Prep time 15 minutes
Cook time 6 hours 30 minutes
Serves 4–6

I love this dish because it reminds me of my grandmother Audrey, whose roast lamb was awesome. She inspired me and taught me how to cook.

Sundays at my grandmother's place were my favourite, because there was always a roast. Sometimes it was lunch and sometimes it was dinner, but of all the roasts in her repertoire, this was the one. It's a foolproof recipe, provided you buy good lamb, and season and cook it well.

She used to roast legs mostly, and my brother and I would always fight for the end bone. We'd usually have a soup to start and then the lamb with roast potatoes and veggies, and an iceberg salad with tomatoes and red onion and malt vinegar. The meat of the shoulder is even nicer than the leg, I think, so it was a real treat when it was available.

When we do our slow-cooked lamb shoulder at Estelle, I always have to eat that little crunchy bit on the end. It instantly takes me back to being a six- or seven-year-old boy.

---

2 tbsp extra-virgin olive oil

1 x 1.6–1.7kg good-quality lamb shoulder bone in, fat trimmed

2–3 tsp sea salt

2 brown onions diced

2 carrots diced

1 celery stalk diced

2–3L chicken stock

1 bulb garlic, unpeeled cut in half horizontally

1 large sprig rosemary

1 large sprig thyme

Murray River pink salt flakes to serve (optional)

Roast potatoes see page 267, to serve

Roast Brussels sprouts with pancetta see page 267, to serve

Preheat the oven to 120°C.

Heat the oil in a large roasting tin or casserole dish over medium–high heat. Season one side of the lamb with half the salt, then place, seasoned side down, in the dish. Sear the lamb for 5 minutes or until generously caramelised, then season with the remaining salt, turn over and sear the other side for another 5 minutes or until caramelised. Remove the lamb from the dish and set aside on a plate.

> It's better (and more affordable) to buy produce when it's in season and at its peak, and lamb is no exception. Have a chat with your butcher and ask for the best new-season lamb they have. If it's milk-fed it should be a nice pale pink, or if it's grass-fed you're looking for a rosy red colour. If you want to truss or tie your lamb, ask for some butcher's (kitchen) string, too.

Add the onion, carrot and celery to the dish and saute for 6–7 minutes, until lightly coloured. Return the lamb to the dish and add just enough chicken stock to nearly cover the meat, then add the garlic and the herbs. Cover with baking paper, then tightly seal with foil, transfer to the oven and cook for 6 hours, removing the foil and baking paper for the last hour of cooking. Now increase the temperature to 200°C and continue to cook, uncovered, for another 30 minutes or until the lamb is falling off the bone.

Carefully remove the lamb shoulder from the dish and set aside on a plate. Cover with foil while you make the sauce.

→

Roast lamb shoulder continued

When cooking larger cuts of meat it's always better to cook the meat on the bone whenever possible. The final product is juicier, the cut doesn't shrink as much and it also seems to have a deeper flavour. Try it and you'll see the difference.

Return the casserole dish to the stovetop and cook the remaining liquid over medium–high heat for about 10 minutes, until reduced to a sauce-like consistency. Strain into a jug and set aside until ready to serve. A good trick is to remove and reserve any fat that rises to the top as the sauce cools.

Serve the lamb in the middle of the table with the sauce, roast potatoes and Brussels sprouts and let everyone dig in. As you slice the lamb, be sure to season it with a pinch of pink salt if you have it.

The most important thing to consider when pairing wine with this dish is savouriness. Step outside your comfort zone and rather than picking up a Barossa shiraz, try something different, like a cabernet sauvignon–based wine from Médoc in Bordeaux or a mourvèdre-based wine from areas like Bandol in South West France, or even a malbec from Benalla.

Serve with my roast potatoes and roast Brussels sprouts with pancetta on page 267.

Starting a Home Bar

By Michael Madrusan,
The Everleigh

Stocking your home bar is like stocking your pantry. If you've bought a jar of spice just for one dish, you've obviously got too much room in your rack. Plan your home bar around the drinks you like to make regularly and, most importantly, drink regularly. If you're into Martinis, a bottle of gin is a grand idea. If you like Aviations but that's the only drink you know that uses crème de violette, you'll need to drink a lot of Aviations to get through a single bottle. And nobody can handle that many Aviations. Buy the good stuff. You deserve it. You don't need to break the bank, but don't try to mix with bottom-end spirits. It won't be good for your confidence as a master mixer.

THE SHOPPING LIST At home I keep one bottle each of gin, bourbon, rye, Scotch, light rum, dark rum, Campari, tequila and cognac. Sweet and dry vermouth stay in the fridge, and there's a bottle of vodka in my first aid cupboard for when I cut myself accidentally. Just kidding. I don't have any vodka. Gin is more interesting. **BOURBON** → Elijah Craig, Four Roses, Michter's, Eagle Rare. **COGNAC** → Pierre Ferrand, Hine. Also try Armagnac for a slightly more punchy brandy for your Harvard. **DARK RUM** → El Dorado 15-year (for sipping), Goslings Black Seal (for Dark 'n' Stormys) and Havana Club 7-year and Plantation Dark. **GIN** → My favourites would be Cadenhead's Old Raj, Plymouth or Fords. Melbourne Gin Co., Four Pillars and Anther are three good local heroes. **LIGHT RUM** → Flor de Caña Extra Seco 4-year makes my favourite Daiquiri. Havana Club 3-year is great too. **RYE** → Pikesville, Rittenhouse, Sazerac, Michter's. Archie Rose's rye is also really tasty. **SCOTCH** → Scottish whisky is a tough one. Find the flavour you enjoy and research other whiskies in that profile. Light whisky (which I call "breakfast whisky") mixes well in drinks. Peated whiskies are fantastic in smaller doses and blended with other Scotch whiskies, as they bring so much personality and depth to cocktails. Starward, a locally made whisky, is a great cocktail whisky. **TEQUILA** → Tequila Ocho, Arquitecto, Milagro. Never buy cheap tequila. **VERMOUTH** → Cocchi Torino (sweet), Dolin Dry (dry). You can gradually build up your home bar with liqueurs and modifiers such as coffee liqueur and Bénédictine. Adding mezcal to your Margarita is an amazing move, and a dash of absinthe in a drink can really spice up your night.

TOOLS These are the essentials. You can collect the other fancy bits as you go. **Y-SHAPED OR STRAIGHT PEELER** → Keep a sharp Y or potato peeler for your citrus twists. Just don't peel too deep and collect the fleshy pith. It's bitter. And never take your eye off the peeler. That thing claims finger tops daily. **MEASURING CUP (AKA "JIGGER") AND CHOPSTICK** → I've got two sets of bar tools under my bed, but at home I still measure with a cough-medicine measuring cup. And my favourite stirring tool is a plastic chopstick. It's light and nimble, making for a smooth, steady stir. I have the fancy ones too, but this guy is always my go-to. **A TWO-PIECE SHAKER SET** → Make sure you buy a good two-piece shaker. We like the stainless sets. But a Boston shaker (glass)

works just fine, too. **STRAINER** → Strainers can be tricky. Yes, you're really separating the drink from the ice, but without the right strainer, you could be letting through a lot more than you need. Ice chips can kill your drink and add unnecessary dilution. So, I must recommend you fork out the five or so bucks and purchase a proper Hawthorne strainer. **JUICER** → I collect all kinds of juicers. But really you can get by with a "Mexican elbow" hand squeezer. I've got a yellow one in my drawer I use for almost everything. **GLASSWARE** → Get started with three types of glassware. Some tall collins/highball glasses for Americanos and Tom Collinses, rocks glasses for Negronis and Old Fashioneds, and some cocktail glasses/coupes for Martinis and Manhattans.

ICE Ice is one of the most important ingredients in a drink, yet it's so often overlooked. Obviously it's in the freezer, but make sure you cover it. Ice that isn't covered will get frosty and start to smell like your freezer, and no one wants a Negroni that tastes like bolognese. Large blocks melt slowly, preserving the strength and flavour of your drink for longer. You can buy them pre-made from a specialist supplier such as Navy Strength Ice Co. (wink wink), or try making your own using the largest moulds you can find. If you use ice from the service station, don't say I didn't warn you. If a drink requires cracked ice, grab a spoon. Place the block in the palm of your hand and hit it with the back of the spoon until it starts to break up. Even my three-year-old, Molly, cracks ice this way. It's that easy.

MIXING When we're talking technique, if you're making a drink, you're making a drink. Give it your full attention, and there are no shortcuts. Much like in cooking, taste your drink as you go. Checking in on your Martini as you stir it will help you achieve the perfect amount of dilution. Store your glassware in the freezer. When it comes to citrus, forget that bottled nonsense from the supermarket. You're better than that. You can squeeze it fresh, and it's absolutely worth it. Lemon and lime are the basics required for all your shaken classics, the other seasonal delights are your choice entirely. We like drinks with pineapple, and freshly juiced ginger gives one hell of a kick. Keep your home bar clean and organised. Always prepare a clean workspace before making a drink. Lay your tools out – you need to work swiftly. Step out your drink, so everything happens quickly: measure, add ice, shake/stir and strain.

MY GO-TO HOME RECIPES
MICHAEL MADRUSAN, THE EVERLEIGH

60ml gin

30ml Dolin Dry vermouth

2 dashes orange bitters

Lemon peel to garnish

THE PERFECT MARTINI

Journalist H.L. Mencken called the Martini "the only American invention as perfect as the sonnet". I always finish my working week with one. This is our house Martini at The Everleigh. In the old books it's known as the "Hoffman House", after a famous Manhattan cocktail palace founded in the late 1800s.

Add the gin, vermouth and bitters to a mixing glass with ice. Stir until the temperature and dilution reach your desired level. Strain into a pre-frozen cocktail glass. Garnish with lemon peel. Smile and enjoy.

60ml good-quality blanco tequila

30ml fresh lime juice

20ml honey syrup

Smoked paprika to garnish

RED GRASSHOPPER

This is a great sidestep from the Margarita. The honey adds a rich texture, while the tequila and lime dance to the song of the smoked paprika. To make honey syrup, add three parts honey to one part hot water, mix thoroughly and cool.

Add the tequila, lime juice and honey syrup to a shaker with ice and shake vigorously. Strain into a frozen cocktail glass and sprinkle the smoked paprika on top.

30ml Scotch

30ml gin

22.5ml sweet vermouth

7.5ml Bénédictine

2 dashes orange bitters

Lemon peel to garnish

DEATH & TAXES

I'm a big fan of combining base spirits. It adds a whole other level of complexity to a drink. This drink is just that. It's rich, complex and perfect for contemplating life with.

Add all the liquids to a mixing glass with ice. Stir until the temperature and dilution reach your desired level. Strain into a pre-frozen cocktail glass. Garnish with lemon peel and enjoy.

SIDES
& SALA

ADS

TAMARIND EGGPLANT
ROSHEEN KAUL, ETTA

Prep time 10 minutes
Cook time 15 minutes
Serves 4

This recipe hails from the Kashmir Valley, where my father was born. Slivers of golden fried eggplant coated in a rich, flavourful and acidic gravy, best consumed with plenty of hot rice and usually some braised dark leafy greens known as haq.

It's an incredibly easy and delicious way to prepare eggplant, and the flavour profile is unlike what you would assume from the region. Kashmiri cuisine is an amalgamation of influences from Central Asia, Persia, China and the Indian subcontinent, resulting in a unique expression of seasonality and terroir. Kashmiri vegetarian food is incredibly special, comprising dozens of dishes created using the same combination of whole and powdered spices, somehow tasting vastly different from each other. Most of the dishes happen to be vegan, as well.

Use long Lebanese eggplants for this recipe, as too much eggplant flesh from ordinary eggplants will turn the dish into an unidentifiable mush. These are available from Asian and Middle Eastern grocers, along with all of the spices required for this recipe. At no point should the whole spices be substituted for powder, or vice versa. The flavour profile of this dish requires a restrained hand for perfect balance. I know it's difficult for some, but follow the recipe. Trust me.

---

2 tsp tamarind pulp

75ml hot water

300ml vegetable oil

4 Lebanese eggplants halved lengthways with stalks attached

3 long green chillies halved lengthways with stalks attached

1 tsp Kashmiri chilli powder

2 cloves

¼ tsp ground asafoetida optional

1 tsp ground ginger

1 tsp cumin seeds

Sea salt

Steamed rice to serve (optional)

Prepare the tamarind by soaking the pulp in the hot water for 10 minutes. Use your fingers to gently ease out the seeds and discard them. Reserve the pulp and water.

Heat 250ml (1 cup) of the oil in a heavy-based frying pan to 160°C on a kitchen thermometer. Add the eggplant and shallow-fry, turning frequently, for 6–7 minutes until soft and golden, then transfer to a wire rack set over a tray to drain. Add the green chillies to the oil and fry for 2–3 minutes until softened. Set aside with the eggplant.

Heat the remaining oil over low heat and add the chilli powder, cloves and asafoetida (if using) and cook for 1 minute or until fragrant. Add 50ml of water and stir to form the beginnings of the sauce.

Add the ginger, cumin seeds, prepared tamarind and salt to taste, then add another 125ml of water and bring to the boil over medium heat. Taste the sauce for seasoning and adjust if necessary.

Return the fried eggplant and green chillies to the pan and toss gently to coat in the sauce. Reduce the heat to a simmer and cook for 3–4 minutes, until the eggplant is heated through.

Serve with steamed rice, on its own or as part of a shared meal.

SOM TUM
TANPAPAT FAMILY, JINDA THAI

Prep time 15 minutes

Serves 4

1 **green papaya** about 850g

Ice cubes optional

2 **snake beans** cut into 2.5 cm lengths (or use 5–6 trimmed green beans)

4 cloves **garlic**

2 bullet or **Thai scud chillies**

5 **cashews**

5 small **dried shrimp**

SOM TUM DRESSING

50g **seedless tamarind pulp**

2 tbsp **fish sauce**

2 tbsp **lemon juice**

2 tbsp grated **palm sugar**

Peel the papaya, then use a julienne peeler to shred the flesh into thin strips. Wash the strips in a bowl of cold water, then drain, transfer to a bowl and let the papaya dry out in the fridge. If you like your som tum extra crisp, add some ice to the bowl.

To make the dressing, place the tamarind pulp in a heatproof bowl and add 50ml boiling water. Set aside for 15–20 minutes, then strain, reserving 2 tbsp of the liquid. Combine the fish sauce, lemon juice, palm sugar and tamarind juice in a salad bowl and whisk until the sugar dissolves. Taste and adjust to your liking: add more fish sauce to make it saltier, extra lemon and/or tamarind juice for extra sourness and extra palm sugar for sweetness.

Using a mortar and pestle, pound the snake beans, garlic, chillies and cashews until lightly smashed, then add to the dressing and stir to combine. Taste again and adjust the dressing as necessary.

> We use Crystal Nuts cashews, which can be found at most Asian groceries along Victoria Street in Richmond.

Squeeze any excess water from the papaya, then add the papaya to the bowl. Mix everything together, scatter the dried shrimp over the top and serve immediately.

ADJARD PICKLES
BENJAMIN COOPER, CHIN CHIN

Prep time 10 minutes

Cook time 10 minutes, plus cooling and 15 minutes marinating

Serves 6

250ml (1 cup) **distilled rice vinegar**

250g **caster sugar**

Pinch of **sea salt**

3 **Lebanese cucumbers** halved lengthways and sliced

1 **banana shallot** finely sliced

1 **bird's eye chilli** finely sliced

Adjard is a pickling liquid that can be used to pickle cucumbers, carrots and other veggies. This is a classic accompaniment to curry as it cuts through the richness of the sauce, bringing vibrancy and freshness, but it is equally delicious as a standalone dish.

Heat the vinegar, sugar and salt in a small saucepan over low heat and stir until the sugar and salt have dissolved. Bring to the boil, then reduce the heat and simmer for 8–10 minutes, until thickened slightly. Remove from the heat and allow to cool.

Place the cucumber, shallot and chilli in a bowl and pour over the cooled pickling liquid. Set aside for 15 minutes before serving.

Serve with my yellow curry on page 150. See page 260 for an image of the dish.

Sides & Salads

"Taste, taste, taste. That's it. Balance the flavours you have: sweet, sour, salty and bitter."

"Purslane is a summer herb. In the colder months, replace with watercress or fresh fenugreek leaves."

ROAST CAULIFLOWER WITH YOGHURT AND PINE NUTS
MATT MCCONNELL, BAR LOURINHÃ

Prep time 5 minutes
Cook time 30–35 minutes
Serves 4–6

The flavour of roasted cauliflower is a favourite of ours at Bar Lourinhã, and this dish has been a constant on the menu for many years. Wood-fired ovens can add a smoky dimension to roasted cauliflower, but with the addition of plenty of spices, a standard home oven will create a great result. Select the smallest, whitest and freshest cauliflowers you can find.

125g (½ cup) plain yoghurt

1 tbsp buttermilk

Sea salt

115g (¾ cup) pine nuts

2½ tbsp nigella seeds

Dash of extra-virgin olive oil plus extra for drizzling

2 small heads cauliflower about 15cm in diameter

125ml (½ cup) olive oil

2 tbsp fennel seeds ground using a mortar and pestle

1 tsp freshly ground black pepper

2 tsp red Aleppo pepper

1 tsp urfa biber sometimes sold as Turkish chilli flakes

Handful of purslane leaves

Combine the yoghurt, buttermilk and a pinch of salt in a bowl and set aside at room temperature for 1 hour, until the yoghurt becomes silky.

Preheat the oven to 250°C and line a large baking tray with baking paper.

Dry-toast the pine nuts and 2 tsp of the nigella seeds in a small frying pan over medium heat until nice and golden (pine nuts burn more quickly than other nuts so don't walk away from the pan!). Transfer to a bowl and, while still hot, add a dash of extra-virgin olive oil and a large pinch of salt. Mix well and set aside.

Trim the outer leaves off the cauliflowers and turn them upside down. Slice each cauliflower into quarters by cutting through the round core at the bottom. Place the cauliflower on the prepared tray, then pour over the olive oil and season evenly with the ground fennel seed, remaining nigella seeds, 2 tsp of salt and the black pepper. Transfer to the oven and roast for 25–30 minutes, until the cauliflower is golden and the core has softened.

You can either serve the cauliflower piping hot from the oven or at room temperature.

Spoon the yoghurt sauce onto a serving plate and place the cauliflower on top. Sprinkle over the pine nut mixture, Aleppo pepper, urfa biber and purslane leaves. Finish with a generous dousing of top-quality extra-virgin olive oil.

CHINESE BROCCOLI WITH OYSTER SAUCE
DAVID ZHOU, DAVID'S AND ORIENTAL TEAHOUSE

Prep time 5 minutes
Cook time about 5 minutes
Serves 2

This is a simple yet effective dish. Easy to make and with a delicious pay-off, it all comes down to the broccoli you choose and the execution. I opt for young broccoli, which is sweet and more tender than older varieties. The key to this dish is timing. It looks simple at first, but the broccoli can be easily overcooked. Take your time with it, and you'll make the perfect Chinese broccoli that is fresh, saucy and balanced.

---

1 tsp sea salt
Splash of vegetable oil
200g Chinese broccoli
1 tsp oyster sauce
1½ tbsp light soy sauce
1½ tbsp hot water
1 tsp sugar
1 long red chilli, finely sliced
to serve (optional)

Bring a large saucepan of water to the boil over high heat. Season with the salt and add the oil, then carefully drop the Chinese broccoli into the boiling water. Cook for 5–6 minutes, until just tender, or cook for a little longer if you prefer softer stems.

Meanwhile, combine the oyster sauce, light soy sauce, hot water and sugar in a small bowl and stir until the sugar has dissolved.

Drain the broccoli, then neatly arrange the stems in the same direction on a chopping board and cut into 5cm long pieces. Transfer to a serving plate and drizzle over the prepared sauce. Scatter with the chilli for an added kick, if desired.

> I also like to stir-fry the broccoli in a wok after it has been blanched. To do this, heat a wok over high heat with a little oil, then stir-fry the broccoli and sauce for about 1 minute.

Sides & Salads

ROAST POTATOES
SCOTT PICKETT, ESTELLE

Prep time 5 minutes
Cook time about 50 minutes
Serves 4–6

1kg roasting potatoes such as russet

3½ tsp sea salt

1 tsp black peppercorns

5 sprigs thyme plus 1 tbsp thyme leaves

1 sprig rosemary plus 1 tbsp rosemary leaves

1 dried bay leaf

5 cloves garlic unpeeled

150g lamb fat reserved from lamb shoulder on page 247 (or duck fat)

75ml olive oil

Preheat the oven to 210°C.

Peel the potatoes and cut each one into four to six even-sized pieces, then place in a large saucepan, cover with plenty of water and add the salt, peppercorns, herb sprigs, bay leaf and garlic. Bring to a simmer over medium heat and cook the potato for about 20 minutes, until tender when pierced with a knife but not falling apart. Drain the potato, discarding the herbs and garlic, and lightly toss to remove excess water.

> If I have time, I leave the potato in the back of the fridge overnight until completely dry. This creates a skin that results in really crisp roast potatoes.

Place the fat and oil in a large roasting tin set over high heat on the stovetop. Add the potato and stir to coat in the fat and oil, then transfer to the oven and roast for 15–20 minutes, until they start to form a lovely golden crust. Add the thyme and rosemary leaves and stir the potato to expose the uncooked sides, then return to the oven and cook for a further 10–15 minutes, until golden and crisp.

Serve with my lamb shoulder on page 247 or your favourite roast.

ROAST BRUSSELS SPROUTS WITH PANCETTA
SCOTT PICKETT, ESTELLE

Prep time 15 minutes
Cook time 35–40 minutes
Serves 6

800g baby Brussels sprouts trimmed

75ml grapeseed oil

200g pancetta or smoked bacon cut into 1cm wide strips

1 large golden shallot diced

2 cloves garlic finely grated

3 tsp sea salt

Pinch of caster sugar

50ml red wine vinegar

Preheat the oven to 220°C.

Bring a large saucepan of salted water to the boil over high heat. Add the sprouts and blanch for 5 minutes, then drain in a colander.

Heat the oil in a large roasting tin on the stovetop over medium–high heat. Add the pancetta or smoked bacon and saute for 1–2 minutes, until starting to caramelise. Add the shallot and garlic and saute for 1–2 minutes, until fragrant. Add the sprouts to the tin and toss to coat in the bacon mixture. Add the salt and sugar, then transfer to the oven and roast for 25–30 minutes, stirring every 5 or so minutes to encourage the sprouts to become really gnarly and caramelised on the outside, but tender, soft and almost fudgy on the inside.

Remove the tin from the oven and add the red wine vinegar while stirring – this will loosen any sticky bits on the base of the tin and glaze the sprouts.

Transfer the sprouts to a serving dish and serve with my lamb shoulder on page 247 or your favourite roast.

POMEGRANATE TABOULI
SHANE DELIA, MAHA

Prep time 15–20 minutes

Serves 8

100g coarse unbleached burghul

½ bunch flat-leaf parsley leaves picked

½ bunch mint leaves picked

½ bunch coriander leaves picked

½ bunch chives finely chopped

2 golden shallots finely diced

140g pomegranate arils from 1 pomegranate

Salt flakes and freshly ground black pepper

Tip the burghul into a heatproof bowl and pour enough boiling water over the top to cover. Leave to soak for 20 minutes, then drain and refresh under cold running water until cold. Drain and set aside in a salad bowl.

Layer the parsley, mint and coriander leaves on a chopping board, then use a sharp knife to finely slice the herbs – this prevents the herbs from bruising, leaving you with a much better flavour and aroma.

> To get the arils out, cut the pomegranate in half, put one half at a time in a zip-lock bag, then tap the back with a spoon until the arils all fall out. That way the red juice doesn't go everywhere.

Add the sliced herbs, chives, shallot and pomegranate arils to the burghul and gently stir to combine. Season with salt and pepper.

Serve with my baked salmon with tarator and burnt butter on page 132. See page 133 for an image of the dish.

PEA SALAD WITH PICKLED SHALLOTS
ALMAY JORDAAN, OLD PALM LIQUOR

Prep time 10 minutes, plus 30 minutes pickling

Serves 4

100ml chardonnay vinegar

1¾ tsp sea salt

1 tbsp brown sugar

50g banana shallots finely sliced

200g freshly podded young peas

Small handful of flat-leaf parsley leaves roughly chopped

Small handful of mint leaves torn

Juice of 1 lemon

1 tbsp fruity extra-virgin olive oil

Salt flakes and freshly ground black pepper

Combine the chardonnay vinegar, salt and brown sugar in a bowl. Stir until the salt and sugar have dissolved, then add the shallot. Leave to pickle for 30 minutes, then drain the shallot, discarding the pickling liquid.

Meanwhile, fill a saucepan with cold water, season with salt and bring to the boil over high heat. Add the peas and blanch for 2 minutes, then drain and immediately refresh in iced water for 1 minute. Drain.

Combine the peas, herbs and pickled shallot in a salad bowl. Add the lemon juice and olive oil and season with salt flakes and pepper to taste.

Serve with my cider-brined pork chops on page 233.

Sides & Salads

Sides & Salads

CHARRED BROCCOLINI, MACADAMIA AND CAPERS
ANDREAS PAPADAKIS, OSTERIA ILARIA

Prep time 5 minutes

Cook time 20 minutes

Serves 4

---

2 large bunches of broccolini
stalks trimmed

MACADAMIA DRESSING

25g macadamia nuts

15g capers

1 tbsp white wine vinegar

1½ tbsp olive oil

Sea salt, to taste

Preheat a barbeque grill to high. Preheat the oven to 145°C.

To make the dressing, line a small baking tray with baking paper. Place the macadamias on the tray and roast in the oven for 10–12 minutes, until golden brown. While they're still warm, crush the macadamias using a mortar and pestle until they release their oils. Transfer to a small bowl and stir through the remaining ingredients. It should taste nutty, sour and somewhat salty.

> At home I have a wood-fired oven and will often cook the broccolini in there, but a regular gas barbeque also works great.

Place the broccolini on the barbeque and cook for 2–3 minutes each side, until cooked through and slightly charred. Transfer to a serving plate and toss through the macadamia dressing. Toss the broccolini with the macadamia dressing, making sure it's well coated.

Serve with my bistecca alla Fiorentina on page 245.

FRIES
DANI ZEINI, ROYAL STACKS

Prep time 10 minutes,
plus 30 minutes soaking

Cook time 20 minutes

Serves 4

1kg yukon gold or desiree potatoes
peeled, cut into 1.2–1.5cm thick fries

1L sunflower oil for deep-frying

Salt flakes to taste

Place the potato in a bowl of iced water and set aside for 30 minutes – this helps to remove the starch and soften the potato. Drain, then pat dry with a clean tea towel.

Heat the sunflower oil in a large heavy-based saucepan to 180°C on a kitchen thermometer. Working in four batches, cook the potato, occasionally moving them around in the oil, for 4–5 minutes, until golden brown.

Immediately transfer the fries to a metal bowl, then sprinkle with salt and shake the bowl to coat the fries. Transfer the fries to a plate lined with paper towel, then repeat until all your fries are cooked. Alternatively, place the fries on a wire rack over a baking tray and set aside in a low oven, while you cook the remaining fries.

> Do not use cutlery! Fries are meant to be eaten with your fingers, so have some napkins handy. In fact, if you cook this for someone and they ask for cutlery, send them home. Please apply the same approach to those who remove their pickles from a burger.

Serve with my double cheeseburger on page 196. See page 199 for an image of the dish.

A Spot in the Park

By Julia Busuttil Nishimura,
cookbook author and food writer

When the spring sun begins to shine and the days grow longer, I adore putting a few simple dishes together and heading down to my local park for a picnic with friends and family. It's always a casual affair and while it does require a little thought and preparation, once you're there, it always feels worth it. I like to keep things pretty uncomplicated by choosing food that travels well and requires minimal crockery and cutlery. Picnicking is such a simple pleasure and in Melbourne there's no shortage of great patches of green to stretch your legs, sip on some cold drinks and share some food. My local is Edinburgh Gardens in North Fitzroy. It has everything you want in a park – great grass, plenty of trees and so many cute dogs. I pack some iced tea, cold beers and maybe a bottle of something fizzy. A stack of melamine plates, real cutlery wrapped in some linen (to use as napkins later) and a few cups, and you're ready to picnic!

"A quick dip is always my first thought when planning a picnic – something that can be served with crisps or bread."

SMOKED TROUT PATE

This smoked trout pate comes together in moments – make it extra fancy with some salmon roe to really impress. To make, mix 400g of hot-smoked trout and 200g of creme fraiche together in a medium bowl. Stir through a handful of finely chopped dill and chives and add in the juice and zest of ½ a lemon. Grate in 1 tsp of horseradish and season with salt and pepper. Transfer to a dish or container and top with salmon roe and extra chives. Serve the pate with salted crisps or slices of baguette.

CHARGRILLED CAPSICUM PANZANELLA SALAD

A big salad for sharing is a must, too. A panzanella-style salad is my go-to – it travels well and gets better as it sits. A perfect picnic choice! For the salad, cut or roughly tear two thick slices of day-old sourdough bread into 3cm pieces. Arrange on a baking tray lined with baking paper and drizzle with 2 tbsp of extra-virgin olive oil and a scattering of sea salt. Bake in an oven preheated to 180°C for 15 minutes or until the bread is lightly golden and dried out. Transfer to a large bowl.

Cut three red capsicums into large pieces, discarding the inner membrane, core and seeds. Place in a bowl and toss with 2 tbsp of extra-virgin olive oil and season with sea salt. Heat a grill or frying pan over high heat and cook the capsicum until blistered and beginning to soften – this will take 8–10 minutes. Add to the bowl with the bread, along with 150g halved cherry tomatoes and 100g blanched, dry-roasted almonds. Dress the salad with 3 tbsp of extra-virgin olive oil and 2 tbsp of sherry or red wine vinegar, and toss to combine. Allow the salad to sit for at least 30 minutes. Just before serving, add a large handful of basil leaves and season to taste. Top the salad with boiled eggs (cooked for 6 minutes, until jammy, then halved) and eight anchovy fillets.

CHICKEN COTOLETTA SANDWICH

Some sort of sandwich is always popular, too. It can be as simple as a ham, cheese and mustard baguette or something a little more special. I usually like to take all the elements with me and prepare them there, so they're freshly made. Picnics of my childhood were either mortadella sandwiches or left-over chicken cotolette stuffed inside crusty panini rolls – both still a regular feature at my own picnics.

To make the cotolette, pound four small chicken breast fillets so they are an even thickness. Dust the chicken in flour seasoned with salt and pepper, then dip into a bowl with two lightly beaten eggs. Finally, lay the chicken on a tray lined with panko breadcrumbs and coat it well on both sides. Shallow-fry each cotoletta in vegetable oil until golden on both sides and cooked through. Allow to drain on a rack and set aside.

Make a quick salad with ¼ of a white cabbage, shredded; 1 red apple, julienned; a handful each of mint and parsley leaves; 2 tbsp of grated parmesan; and 1 shallot, finely sliced. Dress with 2 tbsp of extra-virgin olive oil and the juice of ½ a lemon. Season to taste and set aside.

Halve four rolls and spread the base of each with mustard – I like strong English mustard, but Dijon works well, too. Place one cotoletta on each base and top with a good amount of salad. Spread the top of the roll generously with mayonnaise – Kewpie works well – and place on top of the salad.

MELON SALAD WITH GINGER AND VANILLA SYRUP

I also love to take fruit along with me. Sometimes just a nice selection of seasonal fruit will do, and other times I like to go to a little more effort, such as this melon salad. Any left-over syrup is a great addition to cocktails, too – win-win! Start by making a simple sugar syrup. Combine 100g of caster sugar and 100ml of water in a small pot with a 3cm piece of ginger, finely sliced, and a vanilla bean, split in half lengthways. Bring to a simmer over medium heat, stirring until the sugar dissolves. Cook for 3–4 minutes or until slightly thickened. Allow to cool. At the park, drizzle the sugar syrup over a platter of raspberries, sliced watermelon and rockmelon. Scatter over some shredded mint and serve with thick plain yoghurt or labneh.

DESSE

RTS

BREAD AND BUTTER PUDDING WITH FIOR DI LATTE GELATO
LISA VALMORBIDA, PIDAPIPÓ

Prep time 20 minutes

Cook time about 50 minutes, plus 4–6 hours chilling, 35–45 minutes churning and 1–1 hour 30 minutes freezing

Serves 8

I love making this pudding for dessert because it's simple and uses ingredients that are usually in the pantry already. You can substitute the fruit loaf for any bread, stale croissants, panettone or hot cross buns, so it's versatile, too.

Fior di latte gelato uses only a few ingredients, so it's a reliable way to judge the quality of a gelateria. The gelato makes this already pretty substantial dessert even more decadent, so it's probably better for a winter dinner party than a summer one.

Butter for greasing

2 vanilla pods

500ml (2 cups) full-cream milk

500ml (2 cups) pure cream

4 eggs

115g (½ cup) caster sugar

1 fruit loaf about 500g, sliced and cut into triangles

Boiling water

Icing sugar to serve

FIOR DI LATTE GELATO

135g caster sugar

35g dextrose

20g skim milk powder

5g locust bean gum look for this in specialty food stores

645ml full-cream milk

165ml pouring cream

To make the gelato, place the sugar, dextrose and skim milk powder in a bowl and stir to combine. In a separate bowl, combine the locust bean gum and 2 tbsp of the sugar mixture. Set aside. Place the milk and cream in a large-heavy based saucepan over medium heat. Whisk the locust bean gum mixture into the pan and gently heat, whisking as you go, until the mixture reaches 85°C on a kitchen thermometer and the sugar has dissolved. Remove from the heat and pour into a heatproof container with a lid, then set aside in the fridge to chill for 4–6 hours, but preferably overnight.

Transfer the gelato to an ice-cream machine and churn according to the manufacturer's instructions or until the gelato reaches -4°C and has the consistency of soft-serve ice cream. This should take 30–45 minutes. Pop the gelato in an airtight container and set aside in the freezer for 1 hour to harden.

Meanwhile, preheat the oven to 150 °C (fan-forced). Grease a 30cm x 22cm baking dish with butter until lightly coated.

Split the vanilla pods down the centre and scrape the seeds into a large bowl. Add the milk, cream, eggs and sugar and whisk until combined and the sugar is starting to dissolve.

Dip the fruit loaf triangles into the cream mixture to coat, then layer them inside the baking dish. Pour the remaining cream mixture over the bread, ensuring the triangles are submerged in the liquid as much as possible.

Place the baking dish inside a large roasting tin, then transfer to the middle shelf of the oven. Carefully pour boiling water into the roasting tin until the water comes halfway up the sides of the baking dish.

Cook for about 45 minutes, until the custard has just set and the top is lightly golden. Sift icing sugar over and serve with large scoops of the gelato.

LAMINGTONS
HUGH ALLEN, VUE DE MONDE

Prep time 2 hours, plus 4 hours chilling
Cook time 1 hour 20 minutes
Serves 12

A lot of people hate lamingtons because they're often dry and just crap. So we said, "Let's make a lamington that's unreal."

I worked on this recipe with my kitchen team for four or five weeks, testing the sponge, getting the flavour right and perfecting the cream and coating. We didn't want the coating to be sticky; otherwise you'd get chocolate on your hands when you picked it up, but we also didn't want the lamington to have a crust. Basically, we wanted to make every component great and delicious in itself.

The way this is layered, it's not just two big sponges with jam in the middle. When you take a bite, you get a bit of everything: sponge, cream and Atherton raspberry jam.

Atherton raspberries taste pretty similar to normal raspberries and the two are basically interchangeable. But I like that they're native to Australia and have a slightly more interesting flavour that's more herbaceous, and less fruity and sweet.

228g cake flour

6.5g (1¼ tsp) baking powder

290g caster sugar

80g egg yolks from approximately 5 large eggs

5g lemon zest

40g (2 tbsp) lemon juice

6g vanilla bean seeds

326g grapeseed oil

210g egg whites from approximately 6 large eggs

5g salt

500g desiccated coconut

WHIPPED CREAM

1 sheet silver gelatine

460g (500ml) pouring cream

38g icing sugar

1g sea salt

2g vanilla bean seeds

→

Preheat the oven to 160°C. Grease and line two 38cm x 24cm baking trays with baking paper.

Sift the cake flour and baking powder into a large bowl and set aside.

Place 190g of the sugar, the egg yolks, lemon zest and juice and vanilla seeds in the bowl of a stand mixer with the whisk attached. Mix on medium speed until well combined, then add the oil in a slow, steady stream. Once fully mixed and emulsified, gradually add the flour mixture while continuing to mix on medium speed until thoroughly combined. Transfer to a large bowl and set aside.

Clean and wipe dry the stand mixer bowl, then add the egg whites and salt and mix on high speed until lightly foaming. Gradually add the remaining sugar, 1 tbsp at a time, and continue to whisk until stiff peaks form. Using a spatula, gently fold the meringue into the batter in three batches. Pour the batter into the prepared trays, then transfer to the oven and bake for 13–16 minutes, until the sponge reaches an internal temperature of 95°C on a kitchen thermometer or a skewer inserted in the centre comes out clean. Remove from the tins and set aside to cool on a wire rack.

Meanwhile, to make the whipped cream, place the gelatine in a bowl of cold water and leave to bloom for 5 minutes. Drain and squeeze the gelatine leaf to remove excess liquid.

→

Desserts

ATHERTON RASPBERRY JAM

2.5g pectin

250g Atherton raspberries
or regular raspberries

11g (1 tsp) unsalted butter

135g caster sugar

1g sea salt

SPONGE SYRUP

300g caster sugar

50g (2½ tbsp) glucose syrup

80g (⅓ cup) vodka

COCOA GLAZE

462g full-cream milk

42g cocoa butter

220g Dutch-processed cocoa powder

224g icing sugar

3g sea salt

Heat 2 tbsp of the cream and the gelatine in a small saucepan over low heat, until warmed through. Remove from the heat and whisk until the gelatine has fully dissolved.

Place the remaining cream in your stand mixer with the whisk attached and mix on low speed. Add the icing sugar, salt and vanilla seeds and continue to whisk until soft peaks form, then slowly add the warm gelatine mixture. Continue to whisk until stiff peaks form, then transfer to a bowl, cover and set aside in the fridge.

To make the Atherton raspberry jam, place the pectin, raspberries, butter and 110ml of water in a saucepan over medium–high heat. Bring to the boil and whisk constantly for 5 minutes, then add the sugar and salt and stir to combine. Bring back to the boil, whisking constantly, until the mixture reaches 104°C on a kitchen thermometer. Transfer the jam to a heatproof bowl set over an ice bath. Stir until the jam is completely cool.

To make the sponge syrup, combine the sugar, glucose syrup and 200ml of water in a small saucepan and bring to the boil over medium–high heat. Immediately remove the pan from the heat and set aside to cool, then stir through the vodka.

To make the cocoa glaze, heat the milk and cocoa butter in a small saucepan over medium heat to 60°C on a kitchen thermometer. Transfer the mixture to a blender, add the remaining ingredients and blitz on low speed until well combined. Keep warm if using immediately or set aside in the fridge.

To assemble the lamingtons, cut the sponge cakes in half.

Starting with a layer of sponge, evenly brush some of the sponge syrup over the top followed by half the whipped cream (this should be about 1cm thick). Add another layer of sponge and sponge syrup, then spread the jam in an even layer over the top. Repeat with another layer of sponge, syrup and the remaining cream, then place the final layer of sponge on top.

You can cut your lamington into squares straight away, but because there are so many layers it can get messy and there's a high chance of it falling apart, so we always semi-freeze our lamingtons for about 4 hours.

Warm the cocoa glaze in a small saucepan over low heat. Spread the desiccated coconut on a tray.

Slice the semi-frozen lamington cake into 12 squares, then dip and completely coat in the cocoa glaze. Transfer to the desiccated coconut and completely cover all sides of the lamingtons. As soon as they've fully defrosted, they are good to go!

PEAR TARTE TATIN
DAN HUNTER, BRAE

Prep time about 5 hours,
plus overnight resting

Cook time about 1 hour

Serves 4

We grow quite a few varieties of pear on the property at Brae, along with a lot of other fruits and veggies used in the restaurant. When COVID shut us down in 2020, we ended up with half a tonne of pears on our hands, so I started making tarts and other things with them. It was really a question of, "What have we got?" along with, "What can we sell?"

Beurre bosc pears are originally from France and Belgium. Their texture and flavour are really something. They're very smooth, hold up well to cooking and have a really balanced flavour. And in this recipe, their flavour aligns fantastically with the caramel and the butter in the pastry.

Like many desserts, this one is a show-stopping finish to a meal. It's delicious, and relatively easy in terms of the effort-to-reward ratio.

3–4 small–medium beurre bosc pears

65g caster sugar

40g salted butter cut into 2cm dice and refrigerated

Sea salt

Pure cream (I like Schultz organic) or vanilla ice cream, to serve

PUFF PASTRY

450g unsalted butter plus extra for greasing

500g plain flour plus extra for dusting

10g sea salt

25ml white wine vinegar

To make the puff pastry, melt 50g of the unsalted butter in small saucepan over medium heat.

Combine the flour and salt in the bowl of a stand mixer fitted with a dough hook and mix for 30 seconds on low speed. Pour the vinegar into a jug and stir through 225ml of water. Increase the speed a little and add about half the diluted vinegar. Mix for 1 minute, then add the remaining liquid and continue to mix, scraping down the side of the bowl if necessary. Pour in the warm melted butter and mix until the dough comes together.

Transfer the dough to a lightly floured work surface and knead for about 10 minutes, until it resembles a bread dough – it should feel a little tacky, but not dry. Shape the dough into a ball by folding under the edges, then place it in a lightly oiled bowl, seam side down. Score an X into the top of the dough to help it relax, then cover and refrigerate overnight.

The next day, place the remaining butter between two large squares of baking paper and using a rolling pin to roll it out to a 20cm x 15cm rectangle. Set aside in the fridge for 30–40 minutes, to cool and harden.

Remove the dough and butter from the fridge and allow to come to a similar temperature and consistency (the butter should still be cool). The dough may be a little sticky, so lightly flour your work surface and rolling pin before rolling the dough into a 30cm x 15cm rectangle.

With a long edge of dough facing you, place the butter block vertically on top of the dough and fold the short edges of the dough over the butter so that they meet in the middle.

→

Pear tarte tatin continued

Press the edges together, closing the dough but leaving the butter visible at the top and the bottom. Roll the dough and butter away from the edge of the bench until it is around 50cm long. Fold the top third of the dough back towards you and over the middle third and then fold the remaining third (closest to the edge of the bench) away from you and over the rest of the dough – closing the edges with exposed butter. This is one fold. Rotate the dough clockwise 90 degrees so that the short sides are now parallel to the bench (the dough should resemble a book – with the spine on the left). Wrap the dough in plastic wrap or place in an airtight container, then rest in the fridge for at least 20 minutes. Roll and fold the dough again following exactly the same process – it's important that the dough always remains with the spine on the left at the end of each turn. Repeat this process until you have completed four folds and turns.

After the final fold, let the dough rest in the fridge for another 35–40 minutes, then roll out into a 50cm x 25cm rectangle. Cover, and set aside in the fridge for a final 35–40 minutes. Cut out a 22cm circle, then wrap the remaining dough (keeping it flat) and set aside in the fridge to make another tart of your choice.

Peel the pears and remove the stems if still attached, then cut them in half lengthways. Use a melon baller or a teaspoon to remove the cores and seeds. Set aside.

Sprinkle the sugar evenly onto the base of a 20cm cast-iron frying pan and set over medium heat. Allow the sugar to caramelise to a deep golden colour without stirring – simply swirl and tilt the pan as the sugar melts for 8–10 minutes. Quickly stir in the cold butter, adding a little at a time and ensuring that it's completely incorporated and homogenous before removing the pan from the heat. Allow the caramel to cool and harden in the pan.

Preheat the oven to 190°C.

Place the pear halves, cut side down, in a circular pattern over the caramel and season with the sea salt. Place the dough circle over the pears, ensuring that they are all tucked in and that the edge of the dough is touching the side of the pan. Score the top of the dough with a sharp knife, making three or four incisions so that steam can escape.

Bake for 35–40 minutes, until the dough is puffed up and golden. Turn off the heat, open the oven door and leave the tarte tatin in the oven for 2–3 minutes. Transfer to a chopping board and very carefully invert the tarte tatin onto a serving plate.

Cut into slices and serve with cream or ice cream.

FRUIT COBBLER
KAY-LENE TAN, CODA AND TONKA

Prep time 45 minutes
Cook time about 50 minutes
Serves 6–8

This is my mum's recipe, and one that brings back many great childhood memories. My family are big fans of apple pie but because of Singapore's humid weather, making a pie dough can be challenging. Thankfully, Mum always had this amazing fruit cobbler recipe, which she would make for us on special occasions.

Since moving back to Melbourne, this cobbler is something I bake every year for my brother, Kyns-Lee, and our friends at Christmas. It reminds of me of Singapore and definitely helps curb the homesickness I feel during the holidays. I love using seasonal fruit, and this recipe is great because it is so versatile. I often use berries or stone fruit, but you can also make it with pears, apples or even grapes. I prefer to keep my berries whole or cut my fruits into relatively large cubes so that the fruit retains a little texture and shape once cooked. I also love adding a pinch of sea salt to my desserts – it brings another layer of flavour and accentuates the sweetness of the dish.

350g (2⅓ cups) plain flour plus extra for dusting

3 tsp baking powder

100g caster sugar

⅓ tsp sea salt

110g cold unsalted butter cubed

120ml full-cream milk

120ml pure cream

1 tbsp demerara sugar

EGG WASH

1 egg yolk

1 tbsp cream

Pinch of sea salt

FRUIT FILLING

1.1kg in-season fruit for the photo we used mixed berries

50g caster sugar

2 tbsp cornflour

¾ tsp ground cinnamon

Pinch of sea salt

→

Sift the flour and baking powder into a large bowl, then add the caster sugar and salt. Add the butter and, using your fingertips, rub the butter into the flour until the mixture resembles breadcrumbs. Stir in the milk and cream and bring the mixture together to form a rough dough (don't over-knead the dough as it will make the cobbler topping too dense). Wrap in plastic wrap, then set aside in the fridge for about 15 minutes.

Preheat the oven to 170°C.

Dust a work surface with flour, then add the dough and sprinkle the top with a little more flour. Using a rolling pin, gently roll out the dough to a 2cm thick circle, then use a 6cm pastry cutter to cut out circles. Re-roll any scraps of dough to cut out as many circles as you can.

To make the egg wash, whisk the ingredients together in small bowl.

Toss the fruit filling ingredients together in a large bowl. Transfer to a 30cm x 20cm baking dish. Place the dough circles on top of the fruit, but avoid overlapping them as they will rise during baking. Use a pastry brush to gently brush the top of your cobbler with the egg wash, then sprinkle over the demerara sugar.

If using different fruit, try mixing up the spices: pair apple with ground cardamom, pear with ground cloves or swap the cinnamon in this recipe for a few crushed pink peppercorns. The combinations are endless, so be creative! You can even add a splash of apple cider vinegar for a little tang.

→

Desserts

CREME ANGLAISE

250ml (1 cup) full-cream milk

250ml (1 cup) pure cream

1 vanilla bean split and seeds scraped

120g egg yolks

150g caster sugar

Fruit cobbler continued

Transfer the dish to the oven and bake for 45–55 minutes, until the cobbler topping is golden brown.

Meanwhile, to make the creme Anglaise, pour the milk and cream into a saucepan and add the vanilla pod and seeds. Warm the mixture over low heat, stirring every few seconds to prevent scalding.

Whisk the egg yolks and caster sugar in a large heatproof bowl.

Gently bring the milk and cream just up to the boil, then remove and discard the vanilla pod. Pour half the mixture into the egg yolk and sugar and whisk quickly for 1 minute, until the sugar dissolves. Pour the whole mixture back into the saucepan and stir constantly with a spatula or wooden spoon over medium–low heat for 4–5 minutes, until thickened and the mixture reaches 85°C on a kitchen thermometer (this is called tempering). If you don't have a kitchen thermometer, cook until the mixture coats the back of the spatula or spoon. Do not allow the mixture to boil.

Remove from the heat and strain through a fine-meshed sieve into a clean heatproof bowl set over an ice bath. Place the creme Anglaise in the fridge until ready to use; it will keep in an airtight container for 3–4 days.

Serve the cobbler just out of the oven with the cream Anglaise poured over the top.

The creme Anglaise can also be churned into a lovely vanilla ice cream, or frozen into a semifreddo.

"If you want to glam up your cake, you can make chocolate shards by melting some chocolate in the microwave and then spreading it onto baking paper. Leave to set in the fridge, then break it up and decorate the cake."

FLOURLESS CHOCOLATE CAKE
ASH SMITH, STOKEHOUSE

Prep time 45 minutes

Cook time 1 hour 15 minutes, plus 1 hour 15 minutes setting

Serves 12

I've had this recipe for donkey's years. When I first started training to be a chef, I was given some recipes from different family members (I come from a bit of a foodie family). My grandma taught me how to make this one.

It's one of those recipes I've kept coming back to and it hasn't failed me once. As I've gone on through different roles and specialised more and more in pastry, I've used it again and again. It's a go-to celebration cake. Everyone loves it; it's a cake you can rely on.

Being flourless, it's also very versatile. If you've got someone who's allergic to nuts, say, just replace the almond meal with rice flour. And the cake's obviously gluten free, so you're covering two dietaries right there.

The only tweak I've made to this recipe over the years was to convert the measurements. Coming from grandparents, everything was in pounds and ounces – I can't deal with that, they're weird numbers – so I converted it over to metric for the ease of my team. But the rest is the same; it's a timeless classic.

---

6 eggs

300g caster sugar

250ml (1 cup) boiling water

100g Dutch-processed cocoa powder
plus extra for dusting

½ tsp bicarbonate of soda

300g (3 cups) almond meal

300ml vegetable oil

MILK CHOCOLATE MOUSSE

6g gold leaf gelatine sheets

180g milk chocolate

100ml full-cream milk

375ml (1½ cups) thickened cream

CARAMEL GANACHE

100g caster sugar

35g melted unsalted butter

200g thickened cream

12g glucose

130g milk chocolate

½ tsp sea salt

→

Preheat the oven to 170°C. Line a 20cm cake tin with baking paper.

Place the eggs and sugar in the bowl of a stand mixer with the whisk attached, then whisk on high speed for 10 minutes until super airy.

Meanwhile, whisk the boiling water, cocoa powder and bicarbonate of soda in a bowl until completely combined.

Using a spatula, fold half the almond meal into the egg mixture followed by half the oil, then repeat with the remaining almond meal and oil. Fold the cocoa mixture into the batter, then pour into the prepared tin and bake for 1 hour or until a skewer inserted in the centre comes out clean. Allow to cool completely, then place the fridge.

> I fold in half the almond meal first, mostly because I don't want the eggs to collapse too quickly. If you were to add it all at once, the mix would start to seize up a little bit. If you put half in and give it a little fold, you'll get a smoother mix.
>
> Using oil instead of butter makes a far more unctuous cake. I'm using oil in all my cakes instead of butter right now – it just tastes cleaner and less heavy. If you put butter in this, it would just be too rich and greasy. I'm just not a fan of that. I'm also a bit of a weird pastry chef in that I don't like overly sugary things. I like balance – you want someone to be able to eat all of what you serve them.

→

Desserts

DARK GLAZE

20g gold leaf gelatine sheets

180g caster sugar

60g Dutch processed cocoa powder

100ml thickened cream

Meanwhile, to make the milk chocolate mousse, place the gelatine in a bowl of cold water for 5 minutes, to soften.

Place the chocolate in a heatproof bowl set over a saucepan of simmering water and stir until melted. Heat the milk in the microwave for 1 minute.

Drain the gelatine, squeezing out any excess water, then stir it through the heated milk. Slowly whisk the milk mixture into the melted chocolate until completely combined.

Whip the cream to soft peaks, then fold through the chocolate mixture. Transfer to a piping bag and set aside in the fridge.

To make the caramel ganache, place a saucepan over medium heat and add the sugar a little at a time, stirring occasionally with a wooden spoon for about 10 minutes, until it forms a golden caramel. Slowly and carefully whisk in the melted butter.

Meanwhile, place the cream and glucose in another saucepan over medium heat and warm through, then slowly add this to the caramel a little at a time, stirring as you go, until smooth.

Place the chocolate and salt in a tall jug, then pour in the caramel and leave for 30 seconds. Using a stick blender, blend until smooth and glossy, then cover and set aside in the fridge for 1 hour or until set.

To make the dark glaze, place the gelatine in a bowl of cold water for 5 minutes, to soften.

Combine the sugar and cocoa powder in a bowl.

Pour the cream and 140ml of water into a saucepan over medium heat. Once the cream mixture is warm, whisk in the sugar and cocoa powder and bring to the boil. Drain the gelatine and squeeze out any excess water, then whisk it into the boiling cream mixture. Stir until the gelatine dissolves, then remove from the heat and pour into a large heatproof bowl. Set aside until cold, then skim the skin off the top, cover and set aside in the fridge.

Using a sharp knife, evenly cut the cake in half horizontally so you have two layers. Pipe the milk chocolate mousse over one cake half and spread out evenly. Top with a few spoonfuls of caramel ganache, then place the second cake half on top and gently press so that the filling is even.

Using a palette knife, gently spread the remaining ganache in an even layer all over the cake, then transfer to the fridge for 15 minutes to set.

Meanwhile, heat the dark glaze in a saucepan until completely melted. Allow to cool to 30–35°C on a kitchen thermometer, then pour the glaze into a jug.

Remove the cake from the fridge and pour the glaze all over the cake as evenly as possible. As soon as it's completely covered, dust the top of the cake with cocoa powder to create a cracked effect. Carefully transfer the cake to a serving plate or cake stand, then serve.

CHOCOLATE AND CARAMEL TART
GARETH WHITTON, TARTS ANON

Prep time 2 hours, plus
30 minutes resting

Cook time 6 hours 10 minutes

Serves 8–10

I developed this recipe in 2015, while I was working at the Bellevue Hotel, a gastropub in Sydney. The head chef at the time asked me to create "an epic chocolate tart" for their simple but refined dessert menu. It was an instant hit and one of the first tarts my partner, Catherine Way, and I sold when we started Tarts Anon in 2020.

This tart has easily been our most popular since then, and we can't see it ever going off the menu. It's beautiful in its simplicity, as you'll see from the recipe. It uses a baked chocolate custard instead of a ganache, which makes the tart more delicate and provides that moreish-ness some other chocolate tarts don't always have.

395ml can sweetened condensed milk

1¼ tsp sea salt

SHORTCRUST PASTRY

100g cold unsalted butter diced, plus extra for greasing

200g plain flour

1 tsp sea salt

80ml (⅓ cup) iced water

CHOCOLATE CUSTARD

130g dark chocolate 70% cocoa solids, roughly chopped

310ml (1¼ cups) pouring cream

60g caster sugar

5 large eggs

Carefully place the unopened can of condensed milk in a large saucepan of boiling water, then reduce the heat to a simmer and cook for 5 hours. (Keep topping up the water so the can remains fully submerged; if you don't the can might explode, and we can assure you there is nothing worse than hot caramel splattered all over your kitchen.) Allow the can to cool in the water, then set aside.

Meanwhile, to make the pastry, place the butter, flour and salt in a food processor and blitz until the mixture resembles breadcrumbs. Add the iced water, a little at a time, until you have a firm but malleable pastry, being sure not to overwork the dough. (You won't need any more water – it will be too wet otherwise, leading to pastry that will not only be difficult to work with, but can shrink in the oven.) Wrap in plastic wrap and set aside in the fridge for at least 30 minutes.

Preheat the oven to 180°C.

Gently flatten the dough between two large sheets of baking paper, then use a rolling pin to roll the dough into a 35cm circle, about 2mm thick. Wind the pastry around the rolling pin, then drape it over a lightly greased 25cm x 3.5cm fluted tart tin (this is the size we use; however, any fluted tart tin will work).

Lift the edges of the dough and press gently into the corners of the tin, then, using your fingertips, press into the sides of the tin and trim the edges with a sharp knife. Set aside in the freezer for at least 20 minutes to firm up. (This is also a really easy way to store raw pastry. It will bake really well even after being frozen for up to a week.)

Line the semi-frozen dough with a large sheet of foil or baking paper, pressing it into the corners of the tin and ensuring that the sheet is large enough to hang over the edges.

→

Chocolate and caramel tart continued

Fill to the brim with uncooked rice, lentils or anything similar, then place in the oven and bake for 30–40 minutes, until the pastry edges are golden. Remove from the oven and allow to cool with the baking weights still in the tin (this allows the pastry to cook evenly from the residual heat). Reduce the oven temperature to 125°C.

Meanwhile, prepare the chocolate custard. Place the chocolate in a heatproof bowl and place the cream and sugar in a saucepan over medium heat and bring to a simmer. Immediately remove from the heat and pour a small amount onto the chocolate. Whisk together until the chocolate melts, then add the remaining cream in two lots.

Place the eggs in a separate heatproof bowl and pour the chocolate mixture over the eggs. Using a stick blender, blend until the mixture is shiny and smooth (avoid incorporating any air into the mixture). Set aside.

Spoon the now cool caramel into a bowl and, using a spatula or wooden spoon, work in the salt until smooth.

Once the tart shell is cool, use a palette knife to spread the caramel in an even layer over the base of the tart shell.

Set the chocolate custard over a saucepan of simmering water and stir constantly until the custard is hot to touch, or reaches 70°C on a kitchen thermometer. Transfer to a jug.

Place the tart on an oven shelf, then carefully pour the chocolate custard over the caramel. Bake for 30 minutes or until the custard has a slight wobble in the centre, then remove from the oven and allow to cool.

Wait at least 30 minutes before cutting and eat on the day.

PEANUT BUTTER AND JELLY ICE-CREAM SANDWICHES
KARINA SEREX, TUCK SHOP TAKE AWAY

Prep time 55 minutes, plus 4 hours chilling, churning and freezing

Cook time about 45 minutes, plus cooling

Serves about 20

This is a recipe that brings together a few things that are close to my family's hearts. My son Hendrix absolutely loves PB&J sandwiches and eats them a lot. And we all consume a fair amount of ice cream (perks of the job). If we don't have a few tubs in the freezer, it's like we're deprived of oxygen. This creation is a hybrid of these things and something my son would happily take to school for lunch (I'm just not sure how well it would travel!).

We use jam – typically raspberry or strawberry – for our ice-cream sandwiches, but the classic American PB&J is made with grape jelly. We stick to the Aussie version, as we don't have American "jelly" readily available. (Trust me, it's nothing like Aeroplane jelly.)

Jam and peanut butter are both really easy to make. Peanut butter is simply peanuts and a pinch of salt blended until the oil separates from the nuts and forms a paste. My jam recipe is a lazy Sunday cook, just a bit of stirring and peeking every now and then. Bottle them both up into sterilised jars (see note overleaf). This will make the spreads last longer, and making your own gives you even more cred when making the kids PB&J sandwiches for lunch.

PEANUT BUTTER ICE CREAM
(makes about 1L)

250ml (1 cup) full-cream milk

500ml (2 cups) pouring cream

1 tsp sea salt

3 egg yolks

200g caster sugar

120g smooth peanut butter

TOAST COOKIES (makes about 40)

500g **stale bread** such as sourdough

335g **unsalted butter** at room temperature

300g caster sugar

225g brown sugar

70g glucose syrup

2 eggs

335g plain flour

1 tsp baking powder

½ tsp bicarbonate of soda

½ tsp sea salt

→

To make the ice cream, place the milk, cream and salt in a saucepan over medium heat and warm through until steaming, but not boiling. Whisk together the egg yolks, sugar and peanut butter in a large bowl, then slowly pour the hot cream mixture over the egg-yolk mixture, whisking constantly until fully incorporated. Return the mixture to the pan and place over low heat. Cook, stirring and scraping the base of the pan so the mixture doesn't catch, for 2–3 minutes, until slightly thickened. Pass the mixture through a fine-meshed sieve into a heatproof container with a lid and set aside to cool. Once cool, pop the lid on and chill completely in the fridge (a few hours is fine, but you can also make it a day in advance and chill overnight).

Churn the ice cream mixture in an ice-cream machine according to the manufacturer's instructions, then store in an airtight container in your freezer until ready to use.

To make the toast cookies, preheat the oven to 170°C (fan-forced).

Tear up the stale bread and place on a baking tray, then toast in the oven for 20–25 minutes, until dry and just starting to turn golden. Set aside to cool, then blitz in a food processor to form breadcrumbs. Weigh out 300g and set aside.

→

RASPBERRY JAM (makes about 500g)

500g frozen raspberries

250g caster sugar

1 tbsp lemon juice

Peanut butter and jelly ice-cream sandwiches continued

Place the butter, sugars and glucose syrup in the bowl of a stand mixer fitted with the paddle attachment (or use electric beaters) and cream for 2–3 minutes on medium–high speed, scraping down the side of the bowl. Add the eggs and beat for a further 8 minutes or until pale and very fluffy. Reduce the speed to low and add the flour, baking powder, bicarbonate of soda and salt, then mix for about 15 seconds, until it just comes together. Scrape down the side of the bowl, then add the breadcrumbs and mix for another 15 seconds, until just combined.

Shape the cookie dough into 45g balls and place on a baking tray lined with baking paper with plenty of room to spread a little (I usually cook six at a time). Bake for 6–8 minutes, until lightly browned at the edges and soft in the centre (this is really important – a slightly underbaked cookie is much better than a hard crispy one, especially for ice-cream sandwiches). Set aside on a wire rack to cool.

Meanwhile, to make the raspberry jam, start by placing a small plate in the freezer. Place the ingredients and 125ml (½ cup) of water in a saucepan and set over medium heat. At this stage you just want to heat the mixture to prevent the sugar from burning. Once the sugar starts to melt and your mixture resembles raspberry soup, increase the heat to medium–high and bring the mixture to the boil, stirring constantly. Reduce the heat to a low simmer and cook, stirring every 5–10 minutes to prevent the jam from burning, for 30–35 minutes. To test if your jam is ready, grab a teaspoon and place a blob of jam on your frozen plate. Check the jam after a few minutes: if it's a nice jammy consistency then it's ready, if it's still runny, then keep simmering and test again in a few minutes.

Let the jam cool completely, then pour into a container ready for use or portion into sterilised jars for long-term storage. Keep refrigerated.

> To sterilise jars, simply run them through the dishwasher, then boil them, making sure they are completely submerged in the water, for 10 minutes.

To assemble your ice-cream sandwiches, spread two cookies with a liberal layer of the jam, then scoop a generous ball of peanut butter ice cream and place on one cookie. Top with the other cookie to sandwich the ice cream and squish together slightly. Enjoy immediately. Repeat.

> Left-over jam will keep in an airtight container in the fridge for up to 4 weeks, or for several months if your jar is sterilised. Left-over ice cream will keep in the freezer for up to 1 month.

Baker Bleu, Caulfield North

Desserts

GOAT'S CHEESE MAMOOLS WITH FIG AND SESAME JAM
TOM SARAFIAN, BAR SARACEN

Prep time 50 minutes, plus overnight resting and 2 hours chilling

Cook time 40 minutes

Serves 8

Mamools are sweet biscuits from Lebanon and Syria that are very popular in Arabic cuisine. They're made with butter and semolina, and usually filled with nuts or date jam. The balls are pressed into decorative wooden moulds called tabe before baking, and are traditionally eaten at Easter and Eid.

When I first visited Lebanon in 2014, I ate at Mayrig, an Armenian restaurant in Beirut. It's famous for its cheese mamools, an incredibly delicious version I'd only heard of before then. They came to the table hot from the oven, with a small bottle of rosewater syrup to pour over the top.

I was inspired to make them at home, but I couldn't find a recipe anywhere (it seemed to be an original) and my own experiments never worked, so I gave up.

On a research trip in the lead up to opening Bar Saracen, I visited Beirut again, went to Souk el Tayeb Farmers' Market and bought a jar of fig and sesame seed jam. It was beautiful and made me think how well it would work with a goat's cheese mamool.

When I returned to Melbourne I was insistent on making it happen. After a lot of trial and error, and countless exploding biscuits, I finally created a recipe that worked. It was a very rewarding moment to serve mamools on the second night at Saracen (they were still exploding on the first!), right up until our last night in January, 2021.

I really love this recipe. The flavours are somewhere between a dessert and a cheese board – a beautiful way to finish a meal and great paired with a coffee or glass of sweet wine, such as Pennyweight Gold.

60g Meredith goat's chèvre

40g kasseri cheese available at Greek delis; try Psarakos in Thornbury

Canola oil spray

FIG AND SESAME JAM

250g fresh green figs quartered

125g caster sugar

40g sesame seeds unhulled are best

2½ tbsp lemon juice to taste

MAMOOL DOUGH

175g fine white semolina

90g cold salted butter diced

Pinch of sea salt flakes

2 tbsp full-cream milk

To make the fig jam, place the figs and sugar in a stainless steel saucepan and massage the sugar into the figs. Cover and leave at room temperature overnight. The sugar will partially break down the figs and create a syrup. Note that if you can't source green figs or your figs aren't overly ripe, you may need to cut them into smaller pieces.

The next day, place the saucepan over medium–low heat and slowly bring to the boil, stirring occasionally. Simmer, stirring occasionally, for 30 minutes.

Meanwhile, preheat the oven to 160°C.

Place the sesame seeds on a baking tray and toast in the oven for about 15 minutes, until dark golden brown. The idea here is to take the sesame seeds right to the edge, which adds a nutty bitterness and balances the sweet figs. Allow the sesame seeds to cool slightly, then stir them through the fig jam.

→

"The fig jam keeps well. At Saracen we would make enough for the whole year during fig season. If figs are out of season, you can buy fig and sesame jam at Lebanese grocery stores."

Goat's cheese mamools with fig and sesame jam continued

Remove from the heat and add the lemon juice. Transfer to a bowl and set aside.

To make the mamools, blitz the semolina, butter and salt in a food processor for 1 minute. Scrape down the side of the bowl, then add the milk and blitz for another 30 seconds, until you have a rough dough.

Turn out the dough onto a clean work surface and knead for exactly 5 minutes, taking care that it doesn't become warm. (This can be tricky – if the dough gets too warm the butter will split and the mamools will fall apart during cooking, but if you don't work the dough enough the cheese will explode.) If you feel the dough is getting too warm, dip your fingers in a bowl of iced water before continuing. Wrap the dough in baking paper and refrigerate for 30 minutes.

Meanwhile, to make the filling, crumble the goat's cheese into a small bowl and grate in the kasseri using the fine side of a box grater. Mix together well and divide the filling into 10 portions. Roll into balls and chill in the fridge for 20 minutes.

Divide the dough into 10 even-sized portions and roll each portion into a ball. Using a small rolling pin, roll each ball into a 6cm circle about 5mm thick. Place a cheese ball in the centre of each disc, then cup a disc in your palm and bring up the side of the dough to enclose the filling. Roll into a ball, ensuring that the filling is completely enclosed. Repeat with the remaining dough and filling, then set aside in the fridge for another 30 minutes.

Place a mamool mould in the fridge at the same time.

When ready, spray the mould generously with canola oil spray, then gently push each ball into the mould to shape it, spraying the mould each time. If you find the balls are breaking it means the dough is too firm, so wait a few minutes until trying again; however, if they are too soft they will stick to the mould. It may take a few goes to find the right balance. Set aside in the fridge for 2 hours to firm up.

> You can purchase mamool moulds at Lebanese supermarkets and deli-catessens, but if you can't find one, simply flatten the mamools slightly and use a fork to decorate the tops. Either way they will still be delicious!

Preheat the oven to 220°C (fan-forced). Line a baking tray with baking paper.

Place the mamools on the prepared tray, evenly spaced apart so they don't stick together. Bake for 10–13 minutes, until golden (don't leave them for too long, otherwise they will explode!).

To serve, place dollops of the fig and sesame jam onto serving plates, then top with a mamool. Make sure that the jam is at room temperature – hot mamools and cold jam do not go together!

Footscray Market, Footscray

GLOBAL CONVERSIONS

Measuring cups and spoons may vary slightly from one country to another, but the difference is generally not enough to affect a recipe. All cup and spoon measures are level.

One Australian metric measuring cup holds 250ml (8 fl oz), one Australian metric tbsp holds 20ml (4 tsp) and one Australian metric tsp holds 5ml. North America, New Zealand and the UK use a 15ml (3 tsp) tbsp.

The most accurate way to measure dry ingredients is to weigh them. However, if using a cup, add the ingredient loosely to the cup and level with a knife; don't compact the ingredient unless the recipe requests 'firmly packed'.

OVEN TEMPERATURES

CELSIUS	GAS MARK
110°C	¼
130°C	½
140°C	1
150°C	2
170°C	3
180°C	4
190°C	5
200°C	6
220°C	7
230°C	8
240°C	9
250°C	10

OVEN TEMPERATURES

CELSIUS	FAHRENHEIT
100°C	200°F
120°C	250°F
150°C	300°F
160°C	325°F
180°C	350°F
200°C	400°F
220°C	425°F

DRY MEASURES

METRIC	IMPERIAL
15g	½oz
30g	1oz
60g	2oz
125g	4oz (¼lb)
185g	6oz
250g	8oz (½lb)
375g	12oz (¾lb)
500g	16oz (1lb)
1kg	32oz (2lb)

LENGTH MEASURES

METRIC	IMPERIAL
3mm	⅛ inch
6mm	¼ inch
1cm	½ inch
2.5cm	1 inch
5cm	2 inches
18cm	7 inches
20cm	8 inches
23cm	9 inches
25cm	10 inches
30cm	12 inches

LIQUID MEASURES

1 AMERICAN PINT	1 IMPERIAL PINT
500ml (16 fl oz)	600ml (20 fl oz)

CUP	METRIC	IMPERIAL
⅛ cup	30ml	1 fl oz
¼ cup	60ml	2 fl oz
⅓ cup	80ml	2½ fl oz
½ cup	125ml	4 fl oz
⅔ cup	160ml	5 fl oz
¾ cup	180ml	6 fl oz
1 cup	250ml	8 fl oz
2 cups	500ml	16 fl oz
2¼ cup	560ml	20 fl oz
4 cup	1L	32 fl oz

Carlisle Street, Balaclava

ACKNOWLEDGEMENTS

Thank you to everyone who shared recipes, ideas and knowledge for this book. Your ongoing generosity and enthusiasm are much appreciated – especially so following probably the worst year your industry has ever seen. We're honoured to publish these recipes on your behalf.

Thank you to Mary Small and Clare Marshall at Plum. Your experience and support were invaluable, and we'd be remiss not to thank you for your patience and ability to tie up loose ends, too.

To the TCYK squad – Rhys Gorgol, Sam Aldridge, Ben Siero and Samantha Hogan – we can't imagine working with anyone else. Your eyes make everything better.

Mark Roper, our photographer, and Deb Kaloper, our recipe tester and stylist. What would we do without you? You're a dream team that never fails to deliver, no matter the project's constraints – that marathon final day being a good example. Thank you for giving up your evening with barely a second thought.

To our shoot chefs Sarah Watson, Meryl Batlle and Caroline Griffiths: thank you for your consistently beautiful food and for also staying late on that final day to get the remaining dishes over the line. And thank you Deb, Sarah, Caroline and Emma Roocke for testing every recipe so thoroughly on such a short timeline.

Thank you to Katya Wachtel, for once again giving up personal time to work up the concept for this book and help us understand what it was actually about, and later loaning us your hands on set.

Thank you to Lucy Heaver and the team at Tusk Studio, for editing every recipe with care, and Callum McDermott and Jo Rittey for providing sparkling copy for them to work with in the first place.

Oslo Davis: thank you for bringing so much warmth and humour to these pages.

Sian Whitaker, Bede Dobeson, Raphael Connellan, Ziba Mackinnon and Praveen Naidoo: thanks for kickstarting your hand-modelling careers just for us.

John and Joan Connellan: thanks for giving up your kitchen and lounge room for an entire day and a literal truckload of props, ingredients and equipment.

Thank you to Michael Bacash for giving us a flounder and some sage advice on how to make it look beautiful, and Ash Smith at Stokehouse for making us a cake while on annual leave. And thank you to Severine at Made + More and Meryl at Clay du Jour for providing props for the shoot.

But most of all, thank you to *Broadsheet*'s founder and publisher, Nick Shelton, for making this all possible. Twelve years on, your vision, and exacting standards, continue to inspire us and push us to achieve more.

Nick Connellan, Publications director, *Broadsheet*

INDEX

R

ragu 185–6
ramen, Kyushu-style chashu
  tonkotsu 161–3
raspberries
  Atherton raspberry jam 283
  Lamingtons 280–3
  Melon salad with ginger and vanilla
    syrup 275
  raspberry jam 302
raspberry jam 302
red chilli paste 61–3
Red grasshopper cocktail 253
Red lentil curry 89
rice
  Chicken paella with pipis 189
  Djaj a riz (chicken and rice) 205
  Fish collar nabe 144
  fragrant rice 214
  Hainanese chicken rice 212–14
  herb meatballs 63
  Nasi goreng 156
  zosui (rice soup) 144
rice soup (zosui) 144
Roast Brussels sprouts with
  pancetta 267
Roast cauliflower with yoghurt and
  pine nuts 263
Roast chicken 221–3
Roast chicken wraps 110
Roast lamb shoulder 247–9
Roast potatoes 267

S

salads
  Chargrilled capsicum panzanella
    salad 275
  chopped salad 31
  Melon salad with ginger and vanilla
    syrup 275
  Pea salad with pickled shallots 268
  Pomegranate tabouli 268
salsa, guajillo 123
salsa rotena 119–20
salsa verde 245
Salt-baked snapper 149
salt, toasted sesame 110

sandwiches
  Banh mi 61–3
  Chicken cotoletta sandwich 275
  Peanut butter and jelly ice-cream
    sandwiches 300–2
sauces
  bechamel 186–7
  chilli–garlic sauce 212
  drunken sauce 64
  guajillo salsa 123
  Namamite 53
  napoli sauce 185
  ragu 185–6
  salsa rotena 119–20
  salsa verde 245
  soy and chilli dipping sauce 77
  special sauce 196–8
  tarator 132
  tare 163
scallops: leche de tigre 39
sea urchin: Linguine, sea urchin, tomato
  and parsley 183
seafood *see* calamari, crab, mussels,
  octopus, pipis, prawns, scallops,
  sea urchin, seaweed, shrimp
seasoned oil 163
seaweed
  Cioppino with mussels and rock
    flathead 141–3
  dashi 144
  Fish collar nabe 144
  Kyushu-style chashu tonkotsu
    ramen 161–3
  Namamite 53
  soup base 144
  tare 163
  tonkotsu broth 163
Short-rib tacos 190
shortcrust pastry 296
shrimp
  Nasi goreng 156
  red chilli paste 61–3
  Som tum 258
siu mai, Pork and prawn 77–9
Smoked trout pate 275
Snapper ceviche 39
Som tum 258
soups
  Beef pho 167–9
  Fish collar nabe 144

Kyushu-style chashu tonkotsu
  ramen 161–3
  Minestrone 99
  zosui (rice soup) 144
souvlaki, Chicken giros 193–5
soy and chilli dipping sauce 77
Spanakopita and tyropita 81–3
  Spanish mackerel marinated in
    Andalusian spices 119–20
special sauce 196–8
spice blends
  quatre épices 230
  red chilli paste 61–3
  spice mix 229
  spice paste 217–19
  yellow curry paste 150–2, 227–9
spice mix 229
spice paste 217–19
spiced clarified butter (niter kibbeh) 202
  spinach
  Roast chicken wraps 110
  Spanakopita and tyropita 81–3
sterilising jars 302
stews
  Doro wat 200–2
  Fish collar nabe 144
Stracciatella, walnut and cime di rapa 49
Street-style grilled corn (elotes) 74
sweet potatoes: Snapper ceviche 39
sweetcorn
  Elotes (street-style grilled corn) 74
  Sweetcorn and Espelette madeleines
    with blue swimmer crab 68
Sweetcorn and Espelette madeleines
  with blue swimmer crab 68
syrup, sponge 283

T

tabouli, Pomegranate 268
tacos
  Guajillo octopus tacos 123–5
  Short-rib tacos 190
Tadka 209–11
Tamarind eggplant 257
tarator 132
tare 163
tart, Chocolate and caramel 296–8
tarte tatin, Pear 285–7

Text copyright ©
Broadsheet Media 2021

Photography by Mark Roper copyright ©
Pan Macmillan 2021

Design copyright ©
The Company You Keep 2021

The moral right of the authors
has been asserted.

Broadsheet
Nick Shelton, founder and publisher
Katya Wachtel, editorial director
Nick Connellan, publications director

Plum
Mary Small, publisher
Clare Marshall, senior editor

Art direction and design
The Company You Keep
Rhys Gorgol, Sam Aldridge,
Ben Siero and Samantha Hogan

Photography
Mark Roper, except images on pages
66–67, 203 & 222 © Broadsheet Media
by Simon Shiff; 84–85 & 272–274 ©
Broadsheet Media by Jake Roden.

Food and prop styling
Deborah Kaloper

Food preparation
Sarah Watson, Meryl Batlle and
Caroline Griffiths

Recipe testing
Deborah Kaloper, Sarah Watson,
Caroline Griffiths and Emma Roocke

Editing
Lucy Heaver, Tusk Studio

Writing
Attributed chefs, with additional writing
by Nick Connellan, Jo Rittey and Callum
McDermott

Proofreading
Hannah Koelmeyer, Tusk Studio

Illustration
Oslo Davis

Index
Helena Holmgren

Colour reproduction
Splitting Image Colour Studio

Printed and bound in China
1010 Printing International Limited

Broadsheet
— Media

Broadsheet, founded in 2009, is Australia's leading independent publisher. Online and in print, it celebrates and supports the best of Australian culture through original reporting and photography. Every month more than 1.5 million people visit broadsheet. com.au to see what's happening in their city and get involved with what it has to offer, from restaurants to festivals. *Broadsheet* covers Melbourne, Sydney, Brisbane, Adelaide, Perth and beyond.

Pan Macmillan acknowledges the Traditional Custodians of Country throughout Australia and their connections to lands, waters and communities. We pay our respect to Elders past and present and extend that respect to all Aboriginal and Torres Strait Islander peoples today. We honour more than sixty thousand years of storytelling, art and culture.

A Broadsheet & Plum book

First published in 2021 by Pan Macmillan Australia Pty Limited
Level 25, 1 Market Street, Sydney, NSW 2000, Australia

Level 3, 112 Wellington Parade, East Melbourne, VIC 3002, Australia

A CIP catalogue record for this book is available from the National Library of Australia.

Recipe for Djaj a Riz (Chicken and Rice) (page 205) adapted with permission from *Abla's Lebanese Kitchen* by Abla Amad, 2012, published by Lantern, an imprint of Penguin.

The publisher would like to thank the following for their generosity in providing props for the book: Clay du Jour and Made + More.

10 9 8 7 6 5 4 3 2 1